HISTORY OF THE MORAVIAN CHURCH

JOHN HUSS (1373-1415), by *Hans Holbein*, from *History of the Church known as Unitas Fratrum* by Edmund de Schweinitz 1885

History of
the Moravian Church

THE STORY OF THE FIRST
INTERNATIONAL PROTESTANT
CHURCH

BY

EDWARD LANGTON
D. D. (Lond.), F. R. Hist. S.

GEORGE ALLEN & UNWIN LTD
RUSKIN HOUSE MUSEUM STREET
LONDON

First published in 1956

Printed in Great Britain
in 11 point Pilgrim type
by East Midland Allied Press
Peterborough and elsewhere

To

MICHAEL AND PAUL

PREFACE

BOHEMIA and Moravia, in which countries the story we are concerned to relate begins, were at one time two independent kingdoms situated in central Europe. Later, they became provinces in the Austro-Hungarian Empire. Since the First World War they have formed part of the kingdom of Czecho-Slovakia. Bohemia, now the northern province of that kingdom, lies to the south-east of Germany; Moravia is the central province, lying between Bohemia and Slovakia. The relations of these two countries to each other, and to Silesia in the east, and Poland in the north-east, have been very involved. Many changes have taken place through the centuries, determined by conquest, by intermarriage of reigning princes, and by other factors. At one time (1275) both Bohemia and Moravia were fiefs of the German Empire; later (1345-78) a Bohemian King, Charles IV., was elected German Emperor. In 1364 this King entered into a treaty with the duke of Austria, which provided that if the dynasties of either country failed, the ruler of the other should acquire both; and as a similar treaty was made with Hungary, the origin of the Austro-Hungarian Empire is traced to this arrangement.

Happily, for the understanding of our story, it will not be necessary to study all these manifold changes and relationships in detail. The ecclesiastical happenings, with which we are mainly concerned, were, of course, intertwined with political events. Notice will be taken of these as we proceed with the narrative.

From Bohemia and Moravia the story passes to Germany, then on to Denmark, Holland, England, North and South America, and to many other distant parts of the world. The story of the History of the Moravian Church is, in fact, the story of the origin and development of the first international Protestant Church in the world.

E.L.

43 Glandon Drive
Cheadle Hulme
Stockport

CONTENTS

LIST OF ILLUSTRATIONS

CHAPTER ONE

The Sowers of the Seed

THERE is scriptural evidence of the fact that soon after the Ascension of our Lord the messengers of the Gospel were speeding in many directions, carrying the Good News which had been entrusted to them. Little is said, however, as to their destinations. For the most part we have only the uncertain light of tradition to enable us to picture the scenes of their activity. Even in the case of the greater apostles, Peter and Paul, there are gaps in the story of their lives which still remain to be filled in. Of the activities of the lesser apostles we have in general only the dimmest trace.

It is not surprising therefore that no definite information is forthcoming as to the means by which the peoples in central Europe, with whom we are here immediately concerned, were first evangelized. There are, however, two passages in the New Testament which can be cited in this connection. In his Epistle to the Romans Paul affirms that 'even unto Illyricum,' he had fully preached the Gospel (15:19); and in the Second Epistle to Timothy (4:9) Paul's young lieutenant Titus is said to have gone to Dalmatia. A glance at the map of Europe will show the reader that these two districts lie on the Continent, over against the leg of Italy. From there up to Trieste, a main gateway into Central Europe, and thence on to the kingdoms of Bohemia and Moravia, is no great distance. People in those days were great travellers, and continued to be so throughout the Middle Ages.

Of the progress of the Gospel in those parts little is known for some centuries. One fact known is that in the year 680 Illyrian bishops were expected at the General Council of Constantinople, and that they were only absent because they refused to countenance the worship of images. Another definite fact is that as a nation the Moravians did not embrace Christianity until the ninth century (about 823), when they were converted through the preaching of Cyril and Methodius,

two learned ecclesiastics of the Greek Church, who were introduced by the sister of Bogaris, King of Bulgaria. Cyril is said
to have been the author of the translation of the Bible which
is still used among the Slavonians, who remain attached to the
Greek Church. Until this time the Greek Church may justly
claim them as her sons.[1]

Christianity spread gradually from Moravia to Bohemia.
Many persecutions followed, when the priests were massacred,
the churches demolished, and the Christians driven out of the
country. Some relief was brought when the Emperor Otho I
(962-973) took occasion to unite Bohemia to the Empire. His
design, however, was to subject them to the Church of Rome;
and from that time another contest arose which lasted for
several centuries. In 968 duke Boleslaus II erected a bishopric
at Prague, and requested that Dithmar, a canon of Magdeburg,
should be consecrated bishop. By the command of Pope John
XIII, however, the Archbishop of Mentz refused to instal him
until the Bohemians should abandon the Greek and adopt the
Latin ritual. The Bohemians opposed this innovation, and after
a struggle of ten years they won the concession of having
divine service in their own language, at least for a period.[2]

The contest went on for more than a century, and was
brought to a close by Pope Gregory VII (Hildebrand 1073-
1085). Prince Wratislaus had made further efforts to obtain for
the Bohemians their former liberties. In his reply the Pope
gave reasons why they could not be restored. He said that he
could by no means grant the request for the divine service to
be conducted according to the old Slavonic ritual: 'for, having
frequently searched the holy scriptures, we have discovered
that it has pleased, and still pleases, Almighty God, to direct
His worship in a hidden language.' etc., etc.[3]

Opposition to the Roman rites continued, and it was increased by the emigration into the country of a number of
Waldenses about the year 1176. Their leader, Peter Waldo, is
said to have died there.[4] In private, however, if not in public,

---

[1] Cf. Blunt, *Sects, Heresies and Schools of Thought* (1874), p. 74b.
[2] Cf. Cranz, D., *History of the Brethren* (1780), p. 15; Bost, A., *History
of the Bohemian and Moravian Brethren* (Eng. trans. 1834), p. 2.
[3] The whole letter is given by Bost, op. cit. p. 3.
[4] The date of his death is uncertain, 1197 or 1217 being usually assigned.

the Bohemians cherished their own beliefs and practices for some two centuries. A change came towards the middle of the fourteenth century when, in the reign of the Emperor Charles IV (of Bohemia), an attempt was made to enforce the general adoption of all the innovations of the Roman Catholic Church.

With this object, in the year 1350, the bishopric of Prague was raised to an archbishopric by the Pope and the Emperor; the university having been established in 1348. This was furnished with professors from Germany and Italy, who introduced the Latin liturgy, the celibacy of the clergy, the doctrine of transubstantiation, and abolished the use of the cup in the sacramental service. By degrees, the nobles, who feared to lose the favours and emoluments at the court, were persuaded to adopt the opinions and rites of the Roman Church.[1]

There were many, however, both in Bohemia and Moravia, who still opposed what they regarded as the corruptions of belief and practice which were thus introduced, and who continued to cherish the simpler teachings which had been handed down to them. They were encouraged to do this by a number of prominent men who attained to positions of considerable influence among the people. Among these was John Militach. a master of arts, and a learned and pious member of a noble family in Moravia. In 1360 he was appointed minister of the Castle Church at Prague, where he preached to crowded congregations, both in the Bohemian and German languages. He also established a seminary at Prague for the instruction of young men in scriptural divinity. He is said to have been highly esteemed by the Emperor Charles IV.

On his return from a visit to Rome, whither he had gone to bear testimony against the dissolute lives of the clergy, he was cast into prison by Ernst, Archbishop of Prague. The archbishop was soon compelled to release him, however, from fear of the people, by whom Militach was highly respected. On his release he went on a preaching tour in Moravia, Silesia and Poland. The Pope sent an order to the Archbishop of Gnesen to suppress him; but before he could take proceedings against him the bold reformer had passed away.[2]

[1] Cf. Cranz, op. cit. p. 15.
[2] Cf. Bost, op. cit. p. 7.

About the same time Conrad Stickna, a native of Austria, exercised a similar ministry in Prague. He reprobated the vices of his day, and spared neither clergy nor court. Like Militach, he exhorted his hearers to follow the primitive custom of making use of the wine in the Sacrament. He died in 1369.

Another contemporary was Matthew Janowsky. He had studied divinity in Paris, and became a zealous preacher against the prevalent corruptions of the Church. As the favourite confessor of the Emperor, and having his confidence, he urged him to seek the reform of the Church by a General Council. The Emperor replied that this was the exclusive business of the Pope, to whom he applied. The Pope was exasperated by the proposal, and compelled the Emperor to banish Janowsky. After a short time, however, he was permitted to return. He died in 1394.

CHAPTER TWO

The Life and Work of John Huss

HAVING thus sketched very slightly the conditions of life in Bohemia and Moravia until near the end of the fourteenth century, I must now give a somewhat fuller account of the life and work of John Huss, which is regarded by the Moravian Church as one of its main sources.

John Huss, the child of poor parents, was born in the Bohemian village of Hussenez, near the small town of Prachatice, not far from the borders of Bavaria. The date of his birth is somewhat doubtful, but it is usually given as between 1373 and 1375. His first education was probably received at a school in Prachatice.[1] About the year 1389, when scarcely more than a youth, he went to the University of Prague, where he took his master's degree when he was about twenty years of age. He became noted for his piety, and rejoiced at the thought of becoming a priest. He soon began to give lectures as a public teacher. In 1401 he was made a dean of the faculty of philosophy, and in the following year he was rector of the university for about six months.

In 1400 Huss was ordained priest, and devoted himself to his priestly duties with a lively enthusiasm. His great talents as a preacher appear to have been recognized from the beginning. Two years after taking priest's orders he was appointed preacher at the Chapel of the Holy Innocents of Bethlehem; a chapel which became very closely connected with the reforming work of Huss and the later Hussite movement.[2] It sprang out of the reform movement led by John Militach. It was specially intended as a centre where the Bohemians might hear the Gospel preached in their own language. It is said to have been large enough to contain a thousand people. Already famous as a preaching centre, its fame greatly increased after

[1] Cf. Count Lützow, *The Life and Times of Master John Hus* (1909), pp. 64f.

[2] Cf. op. cit. p. 74.

the appointment of John Huss as rector. A considerable body of disciples gathered round him, and Queen Sophia, the second wife of King Wenceslas, was frequently present at the services.

For a time Huss was allowed to continue his ministry in peace. Emphasis upon two elements in his teaching, however, led almost inevitably to fierce conflict. The people had not forgotten that originally they had been connected with the Greek Church. Only by force and intrigue had they been brought under the yoke of Rome. They still looked back to the time when divine service was conducted in their own language; when they partook of the cup as well as of the bread in the Sacrament; and when also the marriage of their priests was lawful. Sometimes they were reminded of these lost privileges by their preachers; while, on the other hand, Rome continued to irritate the people by further attempts to curtail the liberties of the Bohemians.

Another important fact was that from the first the movement led by Huss was strongly patriotic.[1] In the year 1361, after pressure from the Pope, the Emperor Charles IV had granted to the Germans in the University of Prague (who, as Roman Catholics, might be supposed to favour papal influence), certain privileges and rights which properly belonged to the Bohemians. This occasioned a long struggle between the foreigners and the natives of the country, which ended in Huss obtaining from the King a decree, restoring to the Bohemians their ancient rights. Upon this many thousands of Germans left the city.

In reward for his services Huss was elected rector of the university, and was so much the more hated by the partisans of the Pope.[2] It should be recalled that ever since its foundation in 1348 the University of Prague had been closely linked with Oxford, and that students passed frequently from one place to the other. Intercourse between the two countries was further fostered by the marriage, in 1382, of Richard II of England with Anne, the sister of Wenceslas, King of Bohemia. The Bohemian attendants of Anne became one of the chief chan-

---

[1] Cf. Kitts, E. J., *Pope John the Twenty-Third and Master John Hus of Bohemia* (1910), pp. 40f.

[2] Cf. Lützow, op. cit. pp. 72f.

nels for the spread of Wycliffe's teaching in Bohemia. Sophia, the second wife of Wenceslas, made Huss her confessor, and through her influence he became court chaplain.[1]

The date of the introduction of Wycliffe's works into Bohemia is uncertain. In 1411 Huss speaks of having read these works for twenty years and more. This probably referred to Wycliffe's philosophical writings. As Wycliffe was the most famous schoolman since William of Ockham, it is not surprising that these should have been speedily carried to Prague. It is known, however, that in 1401 Jerome of Prague returned from a visit to Oxford and that he carried with him copies of two of Wycliffe's works,— the *Dialogus* and the *Trialogus*. Upon these Jerome set great value, and by him they were introduced to Huss, who became an enthusiastic student of the works of Wycliffe.

It may be noticed how similar was the situation in England and Bohemia at this time. Bohemia, like England, was being despoiled by the Roman ecclesiastical authorities. The chief offices of the State were occupied by foreigners. In both countries for many years there had been a loud outcry against the corrupt lives of the clergy. Such being the situation any movement for reform must have a dual character: it must seek to curtail foreign influence, and it must deal with the rampant clerical abuses and seek to remove their causes. Both Wycliffe and Huss appear as patriotic leaders, endeavouring to free the country of their birth from foreign domination; and also as religious leaders seeking a reform in the religious situation.

Although at first he had been friendly, the most formidable enemy of Huss at this time was Archbishop Sbinek, who obtained from the papal court an order interdicting Huss from preaching in the chapel of Bethlehem.[2] To this order Huss replied that he must obey God rather than man. When, in 1410, the archbishop carried his hostility further, and ordered 200 volumes of Wycliffe's writings to be burned in the court of his palace, Huss publicly protested. Upon this the clergy accused him of heresy to the Pope, John XXIII, and Huss was summoned to Rome. Instead of going in person, he sent an

[1] Cf. Ibid. p. 82.
[2] Cf. Lützow, op. cit. pp. 81, 87, 103, 116; Kitts, op. cit. p. 41.

B

advocate to defend him. The latter was thrown into prison, and Huss was denounced as a heretic and, with his partisans, excommunicated. The Pope threatened an interdict in every place where he should be received.

For a time the favour and power of the King protected Huss, who appealed to a General Council to decide the issues involved. At the same time he declared his willingness to retract his opinions if, by the Scriptures, it could be proved that he was in error. In 1412 he made his boldest attack upon Pope John XXIII, in consequence of his having proclaimed, throughout Europe, a crusade against the King of Naples and the two anti-popes, Gregory XII and Benedict XIII, promising a remission of sins to all who would assist him in the war.[1] Huss and his friend Jerome strenuously opposed this scandalous measure, and published doctrinal theses against it, thus anticipating the action of Luther more than a century later. The sellers of the papal indulgences were publicly insulted by the citizens, some of whom were executed for their share in the riot. Prague was laid under an interdict; the churches were closed, so long as Huss remained in the city. To obviate the injury which would be done to the city in this way, Huss yielded to pressure and left the city for a time, though he still preached in the surrounding towns and villages.[2]

Only the slightest reference can here be made to many important events which took place during the early years of the fifteenth century. It cannot be explained in full how the affairs of Huss were affected by the Great Schism, which continued for some forty years (1387-1418), and how Christendom was shocked by the spectacle of the Pope contending against two anti-popes. At one time three rival heads of Christendom were denouncing and excommunicating each other in the coarsest language. Papal agents were busy in every country trying to raise money to provide armies which would slaughter the forces on the other side. Some of the cardinals felt that only a General Council would be able to deal with the confused situation and seven of them drew up a formal appeal for the holding of such a Council (1408). A General Council

---

[1] Cf. Lützow, op. cit. p. 96.
[2] Cf. Cranz, op. cit. p. 18; Bost, op. cit. p. 14.

was actually called to meet at Pisa on March 25th, 1409.[1] The main object of this Council was to settle the question which was to be the supreme authority in Christendom—the Pope or a General Council. For centuries the Church had been built up on the assumption that the Pope was supreme. This view was now to be challenged.

Before its adjournment the Council of Pisa decreed that another Council, which was to be regarded as a continuation of itself, should be held in April 1412. After some delay the Council was held in Rome. Even this did not succeed in straightening out the tangled affairs of the Church.

The direction of events now passed largely into the hands of King Sigismund of Hungary, who had been elected to the important position of King of the Romans, with a view to becoming, after coronation by the Pope, the German Emperor. As the temporal head of Christendom, Sigismund thought he was the proper person to set in order the affairs of the Church.[2] He began negotiations with the Pope for the calling of another General Council, and forced him, much against his will, to agree that the Council should be held at Constance; that is, at a place outside the sphere of the influence of the Pope.

The Pope in question was Baldassare Cossa, who had been elected to the papal throne by a conclave of cardinals at Bologna on May 17th, 1410, to succeed Alexander V; who had been elected Pope at the Council of Pisa (1409). He took the title of John XXIII. The most reliable historians admit that before his election his life had been dissolute.[3] Debauchery and unnatural vice were only two of many things which were charged against him; it was even said that he had poisoned his predecessor. This was the man who, as supreme head of the Church, was to sit in judgement upon John Huss and his followers, who had tried to renew the life of the Church in Bohemia.

The famous Council of Constance met in November 1414 and continued to sit until April 1418.[4] It had been summoned

[1] Cf. Lützow, op. cit. p. 95.
[2] Cf. Kitts, op. cit. pp. 252ff.
[3] Cf. McKilliam, *A Chronicle of the Popes* (1912), p. 374.
[4] Cf. Lützow, op. cit. pp. 211ff.

for three main objects: (1) The healing of the Great Schism, and the union of the Church under one Pope. When it was called there existed a Pope (John XXIII), and two anti-popes, Gregory XII and Benedict XIII. (2) The reformation of the Church in its head and members. (3) The extirpation of heresy. According to the statistics usually accepted, it was attended by 18,000 prelates, 2,400 nobles; and 80,000 laymen. Before this august assembly John Huss was summoned to appear.

To induce him to obey the summons the Emperor promised to give him a safe-conduct. Not only so, the Archbishop of Prague, and even the judge of heretics in Bohemia, also gave him a certificate of orthodoxy.[1] King Sigismund had sent two distinguished noblemen, namely lord John of Chlum and lord Wenceslas of Duba, to accompany and protect him. The safe-conduct was expressly intended to guarantee Huss's safety during his journey to Constance and his return home, whatever might be the decision of the Council.[2] Huss set off for Constance on October 11th, 1414, and arrived there on November 3rd, 1414. On his arrival he sent messengers to the Pope to intimate his presence. They were politely received, and given the assurance that 'even if Huss had assassinated his (the Pope's) own brother, no harm should be done to him' while he was at Constance.

The aim of the enemies of Huss was to secure his immediate imprisonment; and to this end they concocted a story that Huss was intending to flee from the city. They prevailed upon the cardinals to send two bishops, the burgomaster of the city of Constance and a soldier, to the reformer's dwelling-place, in order to persuade him to have an interview with the cardinals. Though Huss and his friends protested that he had not come to see the cardinals, but to appear before the whole Council, he unfortunately yielded to their pleas and accompanied them to the bishop's palace. When his enemies heard of what had taken place they danced for joy to think that Huss had so readily placed himself in their power, and exclaimed: 'Ha! ha!

[1] Cf. Kitts, op. cit. pp. 231, 234.
[2] The terms of the safe-conduct are given in Bost, op. cit. p. 16. cf. Lützow, op. cit. p. 184.

now we have him; he will not escape until he has paid the last farthing.' The cardinals gave an order that Huss was to remain in custody. The friends of Huss made a direct appeal to the Pope for the liberation of the reformer, but he declined all responsibility, saying that the arrest was the work of the cardinals, with whom he was on unfriendly terms. Huss was first confined in the house of a precentor of the cathedral; but a week later he was transferred to the Dominican monastery, situated on a small island in the lake, and imprisoned in a gloomy dungeon near a sewer.

The friends of Huss also appealed directly to King Sigismund, who was to preside at the coming Council, reminding him of the safe-conduct he had issued to Huss. He, however, probably never really desired that Huss should be released, though in view of the excitement and indignation which prevailed in Bohemia—of which kingdom he hoped one day to be King— he thought it prudent to pretend to be displeased. He was probably of the opinion that when Huss was removed the reforming movement in Bohemia would collapse.[1]

Our account of the proceedings which followed must be brief. Early in December the Council appointed three commissioners to examine and to report on the case of Huss. These set to work to compile a dossier of evidence against him. Most of the heretical statements of which he was accused were taken from his work entitled *De Ecclesia*. Many of the accusations were plainly false; for example, the statement that Huss had denied transubstantiation, and that he had asserted that unworthy priests could not validly administer the Sacrament. On both these points Huss had repeatedly declared that he held the orthodox view.

Realising now that he was in danger of being caught up in the toils of the canonists, and of a web of audacious falsehoods woven by the unscrupulous lawyer Michael de Causis, Huss begged to be allowed to employ a lawyer in his defence; but his request was brusquely refused, on the ground that, according to canon law, no help could be given to a heretic—though, it should be noted, heresy had not yet been proved, and Huss had always claimed to be a faithful son of the Church.[2] More-

[1] Cf. Lützow, op. cit. p. 221.
[2] Ibid. p. 222.

over, before he had left Bohemia he had received a certificate of orthodoxy from the archbishop and from the judge of heretics. According to Gerson, Chancellor of the University of Paris, one of the leading figures of the Council, this failure of Huss to secure legal assistance sealed his fate.

Attempts were made by the Bohemians to save their fellow-countryman. The nobles of Moravia met at Brno (Brünn) on May 8th, 1415, and sent a lengthy remonstrance to Sigismund, reminding him of the safe-conduct which he had given the accused. A similar letter was sent from Prague some days later by the assembled nobles of Bohemia. A direct appeal to the Council was also made by Mladenovic, a spokesman for the Bohemians. All that could be obtained was the assurance that Huss would be allowed to appear before his judges.[1]

There was considerable delay in dealing with the case of Huss, due largely to the fact that many of the members of the Council were of the opinion that other matters were more urgent, particularly the ending of the Schism in the Church. In this connection many things took place of great interest to the religious historian; such as, the demand put forward that all the three popes should resign; the resolve to depose John XXIII; the creation by him of fifty new Italian bishops; the methods adopted to checkmate this move of the Pope; the irony of the situation when the Pope who had imprisoned Huss was himself imprisoned in the Castle of Gottlieben, where, for a time, Huss had been imprisoned; the escape of the Pope, disguised in lay-dress, and riding on a 'sorry nag'; the final deposition of this wrong-doer, who was declared to be 'a mirror of infamy, and idolator of the flesh, and one whom all who knew him considered a devil incarnate.'[2] All these things, and many important consequences which flowed from them, may be read elsewhere.

In the meantime Huss had to endure all the horrors of a medieval prison. In the daytime he was chained to a post by the hands, and during the night by the feet as well. He was treated by the German guards with the utmost cruelty and suffered from hunger and thirst. The intention was to break his

[1] Cf. Lützow, op. cit. pp. 239ff.
[2] Ibid. pp. 227, 229, 231.

spirit so that he would confess everything and recant.[1] Forty-five articles, taken from the works of Wycliffe, were now published. These had already been condemned as heretical by the Council of Rome in 1412. The idea was that the condemnation of Wycliffe involved that of Huss, no notice being taken of the fact that Huss had often protested that on important points he differed from Wycliffe.[2] Whilst in prison Huss even wrote a tract, entitled *De Corpore Christi* ('Concerning Christ's Body') to prove that he held the orthodox doctrine concerning transubstantiation. All was in vain: the decision had already been taken to issue a verdict of 'guilty.'

According to all the accounts, the proceedings were a travesty of justice. With their many delays and interruptions they were intended only to induce Huss to recant, as this would have an important effect upon his followers and the whole reform movement. If he recanted, the punishment was to be imprisonment for life in a Swedish monastery, in a cell that was to be walled up, leaving only a small opening through which food and drink were to be passed to the prisoner. Failing recantation, Huss was to be handed over to the secular arm to be burnt. How important his enemies held recantation to be is seen from the fact that King Sigismund, as well as the cardinals, urged him to recant heretical views, even if he had never held them. To Huss, who was above all things devout and sincere, this seemed a monstrous thing to do. He would rather die than do this and thus bring ruin upon the movement of which he had been the leader.

I shall offer no detailed account of the final scene which took place on July 6th, 1415.[3] It was made as impressive as possible. The cathedral square was thronged with spectators. King Sigismund sat in royal state, surrounded by the chief officers of the Empire. Large numbers of magistrates and nobles spiritual and temporal were stationed near. There followed high mass, litanies and prayers. The charges were read, including the absurdly false charge that Huss had associated himself with the persons of the Trinity; but he was not allowed to reply.

[1] Cf. Lützow, op. cit. pp. 236f.
[2] Ibid, p. 238; Cf. Kitts, op. cit. p. 39.
[3] Cf. Lützow, op. cit. pp. 278ff; Kitts, op. cit. pp. 395ff.

Sentence was then pronounced. He was to be deposed, degraded and delivered to the secular arm to be burned.

While the sentence was being pronounced Huss knelt down and prayed for his enemies. After his degradation, a paper mitre, about two feet high, on which were painted three ghastly devils tormenting a soul, together with the inscription 'This is an archheretic,' was placed on his head. Thus apparelled, guarded by a thousand men, Huss was led to the place of martyrdom. After he had been bound to the stake, wood and straw were piled round him, and the flames were lighted. Ere he was choked with the flames, which blew in his face, he was heard to cry with a loud voice, 'Christ, Thou Son of the Living God, have mercy upon me.'

So died one of the noblest of men for the truth of the Gospel. But his influence remained to inspire the hearts and minds of the great reformers of the sixteenth century, and, in particular, to give rise to that movement among the Churches known as the 'United Brethren,' of which we propose to give some account.

On May 30th of the following year his friend, Jerome of Prague, embraced the crown of martyrdom, after wavering, as in the case of Cranmer, with a courage and joy that even his enemies were forced to admire.[1]

---

[1] Cf. Lützow, op. cit. pp. 321ff.; Kitts, op. cit. pp. 415ff.

CHAPTER THREE

The Founding of the Church of the United Brethren

FAR from putting an end to the reform movement in Bohemia, the cruel martyrdom of Huss served only to intensify the hatred of the people for those who were responsible for it. The nobility and the people generally were enraged at the faithlessness which had been exhibited. A long memorial was signed by a hundred noblemen and more than a thousand gentry. In this they spoke in the highest terms of their martyred leader.[1] The people showed their attachment to the martyr by carrying the earth from the place of his execution to Bohemia; by the issue of medals, pictures and elegies; and by celebrating the anniversary of his death. The Council met the situation by further persecutions. The followers of Huss were deprived of the churches, and money was offered to any one who would deliver them up for punishment; many were cast into prison, and some were drowned or burned.

Thus began the so-called Hussite War, which for thirteen years was carried on with terrible barbarity. For three years the Bohemians were under the command of John de Trautenau, surnamed Zizka.[2]

Unfortunately, the Bohemians were not agreed upon their demands and soon divided into two main parties, and a number of lesser ones. The most eminent and powerful persons among them, together with the learned men of Prague, were mainly concerned only about the restoration of the cup (Lat. *calix*) in the Sacrament, and were therefore called Calixtines. Another name for them was 'Utraquists.' But there were many others who from the first aimed at a more thorough reformation of doctrine and worship, like the Puritans in England at a later time. Their aim was to restore the primitive purity and

---

[1] Cf. Lützow, op. cit. p. 338
[2] Cf. Cranz, op. cit. pp. 19f.; Bost, op. cit. pp. 33f.

simplicity of the apostolic Church. These were called the Taborites, from their place of assembly for religious purposes, a mount called Tabor, near the town of Aust. It later became their principal fortress. Others were called Orphans, and still others were known by the name of Zealots.

By the Taborites baptism and the Lord's Supper were regarded as the only two ordinances that were instituted by Christ. They considered the monastic Orders as an invention of the devil, and rejected the doctrines of the mass, purgatory, auricular confession, relics, the worship of images, and the merits of good works. They insisted on the exercise of a rigorous discipline in the Church. Their most distinguished teachers were Wenceslas Coranda and Nicolas Episcopius. Unfortunately, circumstances arose which led this party to propagate their doctrines by force.

When Wenceslas, King of Bohemia died, in 1419, the crown was supposed to pass to the Emperor Sigismund; but the Bohemians, who had already refused obedience to the Pope, were not unnaturally unwilling to swear obedience to the sovereign who was devoted to the papal interests. Thereupon the Emperor marched into Bohemia with a large body of troops. The war became furious on both sides.[1] Some of the Taborites demolished the monasteries, stripped the churches of their ornaments, images and relics, and took vengeance on the priests and monks. As not infrequently happens in times of revolution, fanatics arose proclaiming strange doctrines. There were some who announced the personal coming of Christ to reign with the Taborites over His enemies for a thousand years. Then two parties arose among the Taborites, the one more moderate and spiritual, the other consisting of fierce revolutionaries who believed that matters should be decided by force.

The Calixtines, who were chiefly found at Prague, kept themselves aloof from these violent extremists. Their leader was Rockyzan. He was a preacher at the cathedral of Prague, and was held in high estimation for his talents and eloquence. He appears early to have aspired to become the Archbishop of Prague; a position which was then vacant. When the Pope, Eugenius IV, in 1432, summoned a General Council to be held

[1] Cf. Bost, op. cit. pp. 35f.; Lützow, op. cit. pp. 347ff.

at Basle, and invited the Hussites to send representatives, Rockyzan was one of the deputies. The demands of the Bohemians, known as 'The Articles of Prague' or 'The Bohemian *Compactata*,' included the following: (1) Freedom of preaching for their own ministers throughout Bohemia. (2) Communion in both kinds for the laity. (3) The clergy should not hold estates, or interfere in secular affairs. (4) the punishment of deadly sins by the magistrates, and the suppression of the sale of indulgences.[1]

The Taborites, however, were dissatisfied with this agreement, and the war was soon renewed; and now the Calixtines opposed the Taborites. Yet, despite this fact, when Rockyzan was chosen Archbishop of Prague by the States of the Empire, the Pope refused to confirm the election till he should renounce the *Compactata* and give up the cup. The reaction of Rockyzan to this irritating treatment was to try to bring about a reconciliation between the Bohemian and the Greek Churches. In the year 1450 he prevailed upon the States of Bohemia to send deputies to Constantinople to treat on the subject; but the project was nullified when Constantinople fell to the Turks three years later.[2]

For a time it seemed as if Rockyzan would now throw in his lot with the Taborites, and work for the radical reformation of the Church. He was urged several times to do this by the genuine followers of Huss, led by his own sister's son Gregory. He went so far as to use very strong language about the Church of Rome, calling it the western Babylon, and saying that the Pope was the enemy who was sowing the tares of his traditions among the good seed of the Gospel, and that the mass of the people were merely Christians in name. The real Hussites asked him to go farther and translate his language into deeds. They pointed out to him that the complete reformation of the Church involved much more than the restoration of the cup, and that he ought to be faithful to his conscience, and to separate himself from that power which he had himself exhibited as the antichrist. But Rockyzan hung back and gave

[1] Cf. McKilliam, op. cit. p. 381; Cranz, op. cit. pp. 19f.; Lützow, op. cit. p. 366.
[2] Cf. Cranz, op. cit. pp. 20f.

evasive replies. He indicated the formidable difficulties of the situation, and pointed out that by entering into a closer alliance with them he would expose himself to unnecessary dangers. It became apparent that he was not willing to sacrifice the prospect of a bishopric.[1]

Some assistance, however, Rockyzan did give them at this time. He advised them to establish a community among themselves, to edify one another from the Word of God and other profitable books, some of which he gave them. He also used his influence on their behalf with George Podiebrad, who was then regent, and afterwards King of Bohemia, and was himself a Calixtine. At Rockyzan's request Podiebrad assigned to them for an asylum a district in the lordship of Lititz, on the borders of Silesia and Moravia, which belonged to the King's domain. There he allowed them to form a settlement in which they might enjoy liberty of conscience and the exercise of their own religious principles.

The action of Rockyzan in this matter was instigated by his nephew Gregory, already mentioned, who is commonly called Gregory the Patriarch, and who in a real sense may be regarded as the founder of the Church of the United Brethren.[2] He had been a monk, but had left the cloister in disgust. He was the son of a Bohemian knight, and was well-known in Bohemia as a man of high character, an able writer and a good speaker.

Gregory had been influenced by Peter of Chelcic,[3] a village in the southern part of Bohemia. Peter was born about 1390, and had studied at Prague University, where he had become familiar with the writings of Wycliffe and Huss. He was a layman and a pacifist, in the sense that he did not favour the use of force for the establishment of religious opinions, thus differing from the Taborites. The Church, he said, should not be allied with the State.

In the part of the country where Peter's estate lay there was a considerable number of like-minded people who shared his aim of making the Church a body of God-fearing people who sought to walk in the footsteps of Christ. They had fellowship

[1] Cf. Bost, op. cit. p. 40
[2] Cf. Lützow, op. cit. p. 369.
[3] Pronounced "Shellsits".

together, wore a special dress—a grey cloak with a cord round the waist—and were known as the 'Brethren of Chelcic.' He is regarded by some writers as the literary founder of the Church of the United Brethren.[1]

It was men of the character described, and other like-minded men from Prague, who, under the influence of Gregory the Patriarch, about 1453, made their way to the district which had been assigned to them by George Podiebrad. They settled at a village called Kunwald, under the shadow of the old castle of Lititz.[2] The village was almost deserted; the population consisted of a few simple folk who cherished ideas similar to those of the newcomers. For a period their ministers were supplied from the Calixtines, some of whose priests had come to sympathise with the aims of Gregory and his associates. This was particularly the case with Michael Bradasius, a minister of the town of Zamberg. Superfluous ceremonies were abolished, church discipline was established, and persons were examined as to their fitness before being allowed to partake of the communion.

It should be remembered that the members of the society at Kunwald were not yet an independent body. They received their ministers from the Calixtines. Not all of these were in favour of the steps which had been taken in getting rid of Romish ceremonies, and in the exercise of rigorous discipline. Some of these dissentients denounced the changes in their sermons; a fact which led some of the Brethren to stay away from the services. Neighbouring ministers accused them in the Consistories. The Brethren therefore laid their case before Archbishop Rockyzan and his suffragan Lupacius. The latter advised them to choose ministers from among themselves, and the same advice was given by some well-disposed Calixtines, in order that the Calixtines, who did not share all the views of the Brethren, would not be compelled to share the consequences of reproach and persecution.[3]

The Brethren followed the advice given and chose Michael

---

[1] Cf. Hutton, J. E., *A Short History of the Moravian Church* (1895), pp. 14 ff.
[2] Cf. Cranz, op. cit. pp. 22f.
[3] Cf. Cranz, op. cit. p. 23.

Bradasius as their minister. Under the direction of Gregory, in 1457, a conference was called, in which they formed a church fellowship among themselves, based directly upon the teaching of Christ. They assumed for themselves the title 'The Brethren of the Law of Christ.' As, however, some mistook the title for that of a new monastic order, they changed it to 'Brethren', and, later, as they were afterwards joined by many of similar disposition in Bohemia, the designation became 'The Unity of the Brethren' (Unitas Fratrum) or 'The United Brethren' (Fratres Unitatis). They also chose from among themselves three provisional elders, of whom Gregory was one. Later the number was increased to twenty-eight. It was also resolved that instead of defending themselves by force of arms, as the Taborites had done, they would suffer for conscience sake, using prayer and reasonable remonstrances against the rage of their enemies.[1]

---

[1] Ibid. op. cit. p. 23; Bost, op. cit. pp. 42ff.

CHAPTER FOUR

Early Persecutions and Progress

THE village of Kunwald was shut off from the world by a narrow gorge; the Glatz mountains towered on one side, on the other stood the old castle of Lititz. In that little fruitful valley the Brethren built their homes and carried on their daily activities. But even in this remote district they were not long left at peace. The fame of the little community spread abroad. Devout souls in many parts of Bohemia and Moravia, attracted by the reports which reached them, came to join them. Similar societies sprang up elsewhere. Then their enemies got busy and were soon spreading hostile reports about them. Both Calixtine and Roman Catholic priests stigmatized the community as heretics and sowers of sedition. They were declared to be dangerous to the State. It was said that they intended to renew the recent Taborite tumults, and to seize the government of the country.

The leaders were therefore summoned before the Consistory of Prague; and Archbishop Rockyzan, who until this time had secretly assisted them, fearful of losing both his reputation and his office, accused them of separating from the Church, and declared himself to be their enemy. He even urged the King to extinguish this spark of life before, as he said, it should burst into a flame. The King, George Podiebrad, though personally not unfriendly to the Brethren, could hardly be expected to protect them against this combination of enemies; especially since, at his accession, in 1458, he had taken an oath to extirpate heretics from the kingdom. He therefore consented to persecute them, hoping thereby to screen the Calixtines, who had assisted him in attaining the throne.[1]

In 1461, having heard that Gregory the Patriarch had come on a visit to Prague, and that he was actually holding a meeting of university students in a certain house, the King gave orders to arrest them on the spot. Although they had received

[1] Cf. Cranz, op. cit. p. 24; Bost, op. cit. p. 45; Hutton, op. cit. p. 23.

warning of what was coming, most of them resolved to await the blow. Presently the magistrate stood at the door and greeted them with the strange salutation: 'All who wish to live godly in Christ Jesus must suffer persecution. Follow me to prison.' They were soon put upon the rack, and otherwise treated with horrible cruelty. Some of them, particularly the young students, gave way, and made a public confession in the Thein church in Prague. Gregory the Patriarch, now an old man, swooned under the torture, and during the swoon is said to have had a dream in which he saw a fruit-bearing tree and three men. The same three men, it is said, six years later were chosen as the first three elders of the Brethren's Church.[1]

While Gregory lay in his swoon he was visited by his uncle, the archbishop. The latter appears to have been conscience-stricken, for when Gregory recovered he pleaded with the King on his behalf, and the old patriarch was allowed to return in peace to Kunwald. In the meantime the Brethren were suffering fierce persecution. Those in Moravia, who were the first to suffer, fled to Bohemia; but their persecutors followed them. They were said to have forfeited their civil rights, and their property was confiscated. In the depths of winter they were driven from their towns and villages. The sick were left to perish in the open fields, where many died of cold and hunger. Many were cast into prison where, by means of torture, an attempt was made to force them to confess revolutionary designs. Some had their hands cut off; others were dragged along the ground or burnt alive; yet others died in prison. When no confession of crime could be extorted from the survivors they were sent home in a pitiable condition, such as was calculated to arouse a sense of horror in those who saw them.

Some words which had dropped from the lips of Rockyzan on the occasion of his visit to Gregory in prison led the Brethren to suppose that he secretly sympathised with them, and might be induced to lead a true reformation in the Church. They therefore addressed a fresh appeal to him. He gave them a courteous answer, and acknowledged their cause to be good and laudable. But beyond this he refused to go, saying that in such times his credit and counsel would be of little assistance

[1] Cf. Cranz, op. cit. p. 25.

to them. They then bitterly reproached him, saying, among other things: 'Thou art of the world and wilt perish with the world.' These reproaches enraged him to such a degree that he again incited the King to issue fresh orders for persecution.[1] He decreed that all his subjects were to join either the Utraquist [2] or the Roman Catholic Church. Gregory the Patriarch was again imprisoned. Jacob Hulava was burnt alive in the presence of his family, being the first of the Brethren to suffer martyrdom since the Church was constituted.[3]

The Bishop of Breslau, however, interposed and pointed out to the King that a bloody persecution served only to increase the number of heretics. Thereupon the King agreed to change his mode of procedure and contented himself with such measures as would drive the Brethren out of the country. Kunwald was forsaken. The Brethren were hunted like deer and fled into the woods and the mountains. They never retaliated; having taken the decision never to make use of the weapons of force, but only those of argument and persuasion.[4]

When the Brethren first settled at Kunwald they had no idea of passing outside of the National Utraquist (Calixtine) Church. The services of the Brethren were conducted by the Utraquist priests. They had settled on the estate of a Utraquist, under the protection of a Utraquist King. Their main concern had been to enjoy a religious fellowship, based on the New Testament model. To this end, like the Utraquists, they had made use of the cup in the sacramental service, and rejected a number of what they regarded as Romish innovations. These have already been indicated.[5]

Certain changes now took place which tended in the direction of separation. Finding that there was now no hope of a thorough reformation being carried through in the National

---

[1] Cf. Cranz, op. cit. p. 26; Bost, op. cit. p. 47.

[2] The term "Utraquist" comes from the Latin *utraque*, feminine of *uterque*, meaning "both". It was applied to the Calixtines because they demanded *both* the bread and the wine in the communion. The concession had been allowed, and at one time the Utraquist Church was recognised as the National Church of Bohemia, and existed alongside of the Roman Catholic Church.

[3] Cf. Hutton, op. cit. p. 25.

[4] Cf. Cranz, op. cit. p. 26.

[5] Cf. Hutton, op. cit. p. 26.

C

Church, they resolved to take the steps they considered necessary for the maintenance of a Christian discipline among themselves. As we have seen, they had already chosen a number of elders by a majority of votes to whom they had committed the management of their affairs. In carrying out their duties the elders had exercised the authority given them to summon prominent Brethren scattered throughout Bohemia and Moravia to meet in Synod. From these meetings, they sent directions to the various congregations with respect to doctrine, and conduct in worship and towards each other.

One matter about which they felt concern at this time was the ministerial office, and its succession in case the supply of Calixtine priests should fail. Some of these had been unsatisfactory; and the Brethren felt uncertain as to what would happen in the future. There were some who felt that the wisest course would be to act on the advice given them by Lupacius and other Calixtine ministers, and appoint ministers from among themselves. To settle this matter the Brethren assembled in Synod at Lhota, near Richenau, in the year 1467. Some seventy persons are said to have met together on this occasion, including priests, gentlemen, scholars and farmers. [1]

The meeting was preceded by a fast, and opened with prayer and reading of the Scriptures. They then proceeded to carry out the proposal to establish a ministerial office. They first chose twenty men from among the Brethren present, and out of these they selected nine persons of unblemished character and held in high repute for their wisdom and experience in divine things. Of the nine their intention was that three should be appointed by Lot for the ministry. They prayed fervently for the nine they had chosen, and intreated that God would signify His will by the Lot as to which should be set apart as ministers.

The procedure in the drawing of the Lots was this: they wrote the word *Est*, meaning ' It is he,' (i.e. whom the Lord chooses) upon three slips of paper, and left nine slips blank. It was possible therefore for nine blank slips to be drawn; in which case all the nine would be rejected. They then called in a little boy who drew the slips and gave them to each of

[1] Cf. Cranz, op. cit. p. 27: Hutton, op. cit. p. 27.

the nine Brethren. All the slips inscribed 'Est' were drawn. The three thus elected were Matthias of Kunwald, Thomas of Prychelaus and Elias of Kryschenov. To these the Brethren promised faithful obedience by giving them the right hand of fellowship.

At another Synod, held soon afterwards, the Brethren discussed the question whether the three elders should be ordained. To render their proceeding valid in the eyes of the law, and to obviate as far as possible the objections of their enemies, it was eventually decided that the elders should receive episcopal ordination. Realizing that ordination at the hands of the Calixtine or Roman Catholic Church was out of the question, they decided to apply to the Waldensian Church, which was fairly strong at that time in Austria. The Waldenses claimed to trace the succession of their bishops from the apostolic times. They therefore despatched three of their priests, who had already been ordained (one of whom was Michael Bradasius of Zamberg), to Stephen, bishop of the Waldenses. Stephen rejoiced to learn of their emigration, and of the regulations which they had laid down for their religious life. In return he gave them an account of the rise and progress of the Waldensian Church, and of the episcopal succession of their bishops; and with the assistance of his co-bishop and the rest of the clergy he consecrated them bishops of the Brethren's Church. These, on their return, at another Synod, ordained presbyters (or elders). One of the three, Matthias of Kunwald, was consecrated by Michael Bradasius as a fourth bishop. Ten co-bishops or co-elders were appointed to assist the bishops. [1]

Another question which was discussed at this period was whether they should not unite and make one Church with the Waldenses. With the purity of doctrine and the piety of the Waldenses they were well pleased. But they criticised their timidity, and the fact that they conformed to certain ceremonies, which they acknowledged to be wrong, in order to avoid persecution. The bishops and elders of the Waldenses promised amendment in these matters, and embraced the offer of church fellowship. Before the union could be effected, how-

[1] Cf. Cranz, op. cit. p. 28; Bost, op. cit. p. 50; Hutton, op. cit. pp. 28f.

ever, the design was betrayed by some of the Waldenses who were opposed to it, and a violent persecution resulted, during which their bishop Stephen and many others were burnt alive. The rest were scattered, and many of them sought refuge in Bohemia and Moravia, as some of their ancestors had done in the twelfth century. There they united with the Brethren; a circumstance which, along with the fact that they had received the ordination of bishops through the Waldenses, caused the Brethren to be called 'Waldenses' and the 'Brethren of Bohemia,' titles which they carefully declined for reasons which are given in the history of their persecutions.[1]

When it became known that the Brethren had now obtained a ministry of their own, and also episcopal ordination, at the instigation of Rockyzan, at the diet of 1468, a fierce edict was issued against them, and read from the pulpits. They were declared to be outlaws, and the States were enjoined to punish them at their pleasure. During the persecution which followed, Michael Bradasius, their first bishop, was put in prison, and remained there until the death of the King. For the most part, the Brethren retreated into the woods, and hid away in the holes of the rocks. To avoid being betrayed by the smoke, they lit their fires only at night; and they prayed and read their Bibles in the light of them. From the caves and pits in which they dwelt at this time they received the nick-name of ' pit-men ' (Jamnici). Relief from their sufferings came only with the death of the King Podiebrad and Archbishop Rockyzan in 1471. Gregory the Patriarch died in 1473.[2]

Under their new King, Uladislaus from Poland, the Brethren enjoyed peace for a considerable time. Apologies issued by them counterbalanced the incitements of their enemies, so that the King left them undisturbed. Their enemies then made use of a worthless fellow, who claimed to have belonged at one time to the Brethren. He said that in their meetings they blasphemed, vilified the Sacraments, practised impurities and sorcery, and assassinated people. They took this man up and down the country so that he might slander the Brethren and turn people against them. At last, however, he confessed that

---

[1] Cf. Cranz, op. cit. pp. 29f.; Bost, op. cit. p. 51.
[2] Cf. Cranz, op. cit. p. 30; Hutton, op. cit. p. 29.

he had lied, and that he knew nothing against these people.[1]

Further action was taken against the Brethren in 1481. On the death of King Podiebrad Matthias, King of Hungary, had seized upon Bohemia, Moravia, Lusatia and Silesia. The Brethren were banished from Moravia, and some of them emigrated through Hungary and Transylvania into Moldavia; but at the end of six years they returned to their own country. During this period the Brethren in Bohemia had a season of calm.[2]

One of the outstanding personalities of this period was known as Luke of Prague. He was born about 1460, and graduated as a bachelor of Prague University. He became a deeply-read scholar, and for some forty years he exercised a great influence among the Brethren. He found a warm supporter in Procop of Neuhaus, who also was a graduate of the university. Both were inspired by liberal ideas. Not all the Brethren agreed with these, and an opposition party was led by two farmers, named Amos and Jacob. Luke and his followers, however, won the day; and it was decided that the writings of Peter of Chelcic and Gregory the Patriarch should no longer be regarded as binding upon the Brethren. It was declared to be sufficient to follow the teachings of the Scripture. Luke also enlarged the number of bishops and became one himself. Much was done to beautify the services. Singing was encouraged, and a certain amount of ritual was introduced.[3]

Though the printing-press was still in its very early days, Luke made much use of it. It is claimed that the Brethren were the first people in Europe to have the Bible printed in their own language. This was printed in Venice. So quick was the sale that two new editions were shortly after printed at Nuremberg. Soon afterwards three printing-presses of their own were established: one at Prague, another at Bunzlau in Bohemia, and a third at Kralitz in Moravia, where at first nothing was printed but Bohemian Bibles. This translation, made from the Vulgate, served the Brethren for a hundred years. Then a new translation from the original text was undertaken

---

[1] Cf. Cranz, op. cit. p. 31.
[2] Cf. Bost, op. cit. p. 56.
[3] Cf. Hutton, op. cit. pp. 3of.

by bishop John Aeneas and his assistants, at the expense of baron John Sherotin. [1]

The severest persecutions at this period came from the Calixtines, who, excepting for the use of the cup in the Sacrament, were little different from the Roman Catholics. They sent their priests for ordination to Italy, where they gave themselves out for Romish clergy. Their hatred was due to the fact that the Brethren had separated from them and, by a purer doctrine and a better life, put them to shame. They had their own ministry, and formed separate congregations. The King was intent upon bringing about a religious peace between the Roman Catholics and the Calixtines, in which case the latter were to have the *Compactata* and various church privileges confirmed to them by the Pope. These were postponed from time to time, it was said, because of the discord which prevailed among the Bohemians, and because they tolerated the Waldensians in their midst. When mild intreaties and various conferences failed to achieve the unity desired coercive measures were adopted.

The Brethren were not lovers of separation for its own sake, as was shown by their actions on several occasions. In 1474, for example, and again in 1489 they sent out deputies, with a passport from the King, to examine into the state of Christendom, the aim being to see if there were any living Church to be found in any part, free from errors and superstition, and regulated according to Christ's plan and rule. They went to Greece and Dalmatia, to Moscovia and Scythia, to Palestine and Egypt, to Constantinople and Thrace, to Rome, Italy and France. They met with many pious souls, especially among the Waldenses, who sighed for better things. They saw several burnt alive for the truth. But nowhere could they find a congregation which they could join. Their dislike of schism, however, found expression in a resolution passed at a Synod at this period to the effect: ' That, if God should, anywhere in the world, awake genuine ministers and reformers in the Church they would make a common cause with them.'[3]

[1] Cf. Cranz, op. cit. p. 36; Bost, op. cit. p. 57.
[2] Cf. Cranz, op. cit. pp. 36f.
[3] Cf. Cranz, op. cit. p. 38.

In the year 1500 Pope Alexander VI sent an agent into Bohemia to preach against the Brethren, and a certain Dr. Augustin urged the King to destroy 'these shameless vagabonds.' In consequence, in 1507, he issued the Edict of St. James against the Brethren. Their meetings were forbidden, and their books and tracts were burnt. A merciless persecution began. All the Brethren who refused to join either the Utraquist or Roman Church were to be immediately expelled the country. Some were imprisoned, others tortured, and a number were burnt at the stake.[1]

In this time of hardship and danger (1507-1527) bishop Luke of Prague was a true leader and pastor of God's people. He travelled from settlement to settlement, held services wherever he could within or out of doors, and repeatedly wrote letters to the King. At length he fell into the hands of a robber knight, called Peter Suda (c. 1515). He was cast into a dungeon, loaded with chains, and threatened with torture and the stake. Some relief came when certain of the more resolute of the enemies of the Brethren died sudden deaths. Luke of Prague was set free. Uladislaus of Bohemia also died, and a boy was set upon the throne. The Utraquists and Roman Catholics began to quarrel with each other, and in the confusion the Brethren were allowed to live in peace. Bishop Luke died in the Brethren's House of Jungbunzlau in 1528.[2]

We are now in the early years of the sixteenth century and the period of the Reformation, as it is usually called, is in sight. Before going on to speak of the relations which were established between the Brethren and Luther, Calvin and the other great Reformers, it may be helpful to indicate very briefly the general position of the Brethren's Church at this time. Despite all the machinations of their enemies, and all the imprisonments and burnings which had taken place, their churches had continually multiplied. At the beginning of the sixteenth century, and before Luther and Calvin had become generally known, it is claimed that in Bohemia and Moravia there were two hundred societies, regularly and fully constituted as Protestant churches.

[1] Cf. Hutton, op. cit. p. 34.
[2] Cf. Hutton, op. cit. pp. 36f., 38f.

In the meantime, the Calixtines, who, as we have seen, apart from the use of the cup, were practically Roman Catholics, when the Protestants were driven out of Bohemia became increasingly mixed up with the Roman Catholic party.

When the Brethren heard of the attempts that were being made by Erasmus of Rotterdam to improve the life of the Roman Church, in 1511, they sent him a copy of the confession which they had presented to King Uladislaus in 1508. They requested that he should examine it and, if he discovered any errors, should point them out; if not, they asked him to testify to the truth of their doctrine. He excused himself from doing this on account of his many occupations. He also stated that his testimony would serve only to endanger himself rather than deliver them from their adversaries. This temporizing reply notwithstanding, Erasmus, on various occasions, when he could do so without risk to himself, bore high testimony to their sentiments and conduct. An illustration of this is found in his Preface to the New Testament. [1]

---

[1] Cf. Bost, op. cit. p. 67; Cranz, op. cit. pp. 38f.

CHAPTER FIVE

The Brethren and the Reformation

A HUNDRED years had now passed since the martyrdom of John Huss in 1415. One of the last statements made by him to his judges was in these words: 'A hundred years hence you shall answer for this before God and me.' [1] The words were remembered; and the time had now come when this forecast was to receive a remarkable fulfilment. Martin Luther (1483-1546) had begun to preach against the errors of Rome, and particularly against the scandal of the sale of indulgences. In the year 1517 he had nailed his ninty-five theses against indulgences to the door of the Castle Church in the small town of Wittenberg in Saxony. [2] We have already noticed the anxious search which the Brethren had repeatedly made in many directions for people who would live their lives in accordance with the teaching of the Gospel, and administer scriptural discipline; and likewise their resolve, if such could be found, ' to make common cause with them.' We can therefore imagine with what joy they heard of Luther's bold testimony to the truth. and of the success which was attending upon his labours.

In the year 1522 two of the Brethren were sent to assure Luther of the deep interest they felt in the work he was doing, and of their prayers that this would continue to be successful. At the same time they gave him an account of their own doctrine and constitution. Luther received them with kindness, and afterwards declared that though he had previously felt a strong prejudice against the Brethren, after a perusal of their writings he was now quite of another mind. In the year following, the Brethren wrote to him again, this time urging that in his work order and discipline should go hand-in-hand with sound doctrine. In 1524 they made a further inquiry into this

[1] Cf. Cranz, op. cit. p. 42.
[2] On these see Lindsay, T. M., *History of the Reformation.* vol. i. (1909), pp. 228ff.

matter, and at the same time pointed out that his failure to establish a rigorous discipline was operating against the Brethren's Church; since some of their congregation, who were not yet sufficiently grounded in the faith, were minded to withdraw from their community, under the pretext that among the followers of Luther they could enjoy the Gospel without such close discipline. Luther appears to have been somewhat annoyed by this plain speaking, and he made certain complaints against the Brethren. [1]

Soon, however, such feelings were allayed. In 1532 they sent him the confession of faith which they had delivered to George, the Margrave of Brandenburg, the guardian of King Lewis. He caused this to be printed at Wittenberg in 1533, with a Preface by himself, in which he bore a fine testimony to the Brethren. In this he declared that his jealousy had now passed away. Among other things, he said: ' While I was a papist, my zeal for religion made me cordially hate the Brethren, and consequently likewise, the writings of Huss . . . . But since God hath discovered to me the ' son of perdition,' I think otherwise, and am constrained to honour those as saints and martyrs whom the pope condemned and murdered as heretics; for they died for the truth of their testimony . . . . We sincerely rejoice, both for their sakes and ours, that the suspicion which heretofore alienated us, has been removed, and that we are now gathered into one fold, under the only Shepherd and Bishop of our souls, to whom be glory to all eternity, Amen.' [2]

In 1535, in conjunction with Melanchthon, he wrote to them, saying, among other things: ' Since we are agreed in the principal articles of the Christian doctrine, let us receive one another in love; nor shall any differences of usages and ceremonies disunite our hearts.' A third deputation followed in 1536, in which the Brethren continued to press the matter of a better church discipline. Luther replied that at that time, and under the circumstances then existing, he could go no further.

As various reports concerning the laxity of church dis-

---

[1] Cf. Bost, op. cit. pp. 68ff.; Cranz, op. cit. p. 43.
[2] Cf. Cranz, op. cit. p. 43; Bost, op. cit. pp. 68f.

cipline among the Lutherans continued to reach the Brethren, they resolved to send deputies to see things for themselves. These stayed a month at Wittenberg. They had much conference with Luther and Melanchthon concerning church discipline. In the year 1540 they sent John Augusta, one of their most prominent and respected elders, to Luther; and in 1542 the same elder, along with George Israel, another of their best known elders, went to visit Luther for the last time. On each occasion the object of their visit was to stress the need for a better church discipline. Luther acknowledged the need for this, and promised that as soon as the Church should be more settled he would attend to it. When they took leave of him, in the presence of other professors of the University, he gave them the right hand of fellowship, and said: ' Be diligent in promoting the work of Christ among your countrymen; we will do the same according to our ability among the Germans.' [1]

From Strasburg also there came letters of inquiry concerning the Brethren's doctrine and discipline: from Fabricius Capito in 1533, and from Martin Bucer in 1540. In response, the Brethren sent Matthias Erythreus to give them the desired information. This delighted the Reformers so much that Bucer burst into tears, in the presence of the other divines of Strasburg, and wrote to the Brethren, saying, ' I believe ye are the only people at this day, who, together with a pure doctrine, exercise a genuine and well-adapted discipline, which is not grievous, but profitable.'

John Calvin, then minister of the Church of the French refugees at Strasburg, likewise became acquainted with the Brethren, and kept up a considerable correspondence with them. In carrying out the reformation of the Church in Geneva he is said to have introduced several of their church orders into his church constitution. [2]

On the death of Luther, in 1546, the Bohemians became involved in the War of Smalcald. In this war France and Spain united to crush the Protestants of France, beginning with the Waldenses. On the other hand, the Emperor of Germany, Charles V, and Ferdinand, King of Bohemia, joined forces

[1] Cf. Cranz, op. cit. p. 44; Bost, op. cit. p. 72.
[2] Cf. Cranz, op. cit. p. 45.

against the Protestants of their States. The Bohemian nation refused to fight against the Elector of Saxony, who was considered as the protector of the reformed religion. The Brethren were held to be largely responsible for the attitude of the Bohemians; and, on account of their frequent deputations to, and correspondence with, Luther, they were accused of having plotted to place the Elector of Saxony on the throne of Bohemia.[1]

On this account Ferdinand resolved to punish them. Several of their principal people were banished. Others were imprisoned, and their estates were confiscated. John Augusta, their chief elder, and certain others were placed upon the rack three times, with a view to the extortion of a confession of the alleged plots. John Augusta was kept in prison for sixteen years, and only released on the death of Ferdinand. The churches of the Brethren were closed, and their ministers persecuted. The people were commanded to join either the Roman Church or the Calixtine. Failing this, they were to leave the country within six weeks. Some of them joined the Calixtines; but the greater part emigrated to Poland in 1548, under the care of their bishop, Matthias Syon. At first they were kindly received; but after about ten weeks they were banished by the King, at the instigation of the Roman Catholic bishop of Posen.

Thence they passed into Prussia, where duke Albert gave them a kindly reception. When an attempt was made to cast suspicion upon their doctrine, the King ordered them to be examined by five Lutheran ministers of Königsberg. Finding that their doctrines agreed with the Confession of Augsburg, a diploma was issued, dated 9th of March, 1549, according to which the government granted them all the privileges of citizens, and assigned them seven townships as their places of residence. They received great assistance from Paul Speratus, the celebrated bishop of Pomerania.[2]

The progress and experiences of the Brethren in Poland and Prussia lie outside our main theme, and will here be treated very briefly. Only a few matters of special interest will be mentioned. Though the Brethren as a body spent so short a

[1] Ibid. p. 46.
[2] Cf. Cranz, op. cit. pp. 46f.; Bost, op. cit. pp. 75f.

time in Poland, their testimony produced a considerable result. Many of the nobles and citizens received their message with joy. Certain of the pastors who were settled in Prussia visited Poland from time to time to encourage and confirm the converts. One of the greatest leaders of the Brethren at this time was George Israel, son of a blacksmith, a young man of thirty. Already he had been in prison in the White Tower of Prague, but had escaped and joined the Brethren in Poland, where he exercised a great influence, being able to speak Polish. Though he went to East Prussia, he soon returned to Poland, travelling alone on horseback. He reached Posen, the capital of Greater Poland, where he assumed many disguises, and held secret meetings. One of his converts was count Ostrorog, who dismissed his court chaplain and installed George Israel in his place. The town of Ostrorog soon became the centre of the Brethren's work in Poland. Before seven years had passed the Brethren had established forty congregations in this, their first land of exile. [1]

In Poland at this time the Protestants were divided into three different sections or parties—the Lutherans, the Reformed or Calvinists, and the Brethren. Suggestions were made that these should be united to form one Protestant Church. Councils and Synods and United Synods were held to consider the matter. These went on for some fifteen years. Each Church, however, wanted to be the leading Church in Poland. The situation became urgent when it was perceived that the Jesuits were regaining ground. At last, in 1570, the Brethren, who had taken the lead in these deliberations, persuaded the representatives to meet in the great United Synod of Sendomir, the largest Synod ever held in Poland. The aim was to bring all Protestants into one body or Church. The Calvinists were the strongest force, and after them the Lutherans; whereas the Brethren claimed that they were the oldest Protestant Church in Europe. Each of the parties urged the claims of their own constitution as the basis of the proposed United Church. For a time there was a deadlock. The chief endeavour of each party was not so much to effect a union as to draw over the others to its side.

Soon, however, it was perceived that harmony might well

[1] Cf. Cranz, op. cit. p. 50; Hutton, op. cit. pp. 58f.

subsist among them while each retained its own confession;
and, in fact, that union could take place upon no other principle. They therefore came to the following resolution:- That, as
their confessions agreed in all essential points of doctrine, they
would consider each other as of the same household of faith;
love as brethren; and render to each other mutual services,
though they might differ in outward forms.

They added to this, that the members of one communion
should not only have fellowship with the rest in the preaching
of the Word, but also at the Lord's Supper; and that, in token
of their union, each of the three Churches should send a certain number of deputies to the General Synods which might
be held by their brethren of another profession, at any time
or place appointed. [1]

The articles of this union, which received the name of con-
sensus, having been reduced to writing, and read in the full
assembly, all the members of the Synod promised faithfully to
obey them. They then joined hands and sang the *Te Deum*.

At the Synod of Posen, in 1582, attempts were made to dis-
turb the union thus achieved, particularly by two Lutheran
preachers; namely Paul Gerike and Enoch. The matter was carried forward to the Synod of Thorn in 1595. As Gerike would
listen to no compromise he was deposed from his office. Until
his death, in 1603, Gliczner, the Lutheran superintendent, was
able to retain the Lutherans within the United Church. But his
successors, holding different views, allowed the fellowship with
the other communions to be interrupted for a century. The
members of the Reformed Church and the Brethren continued
to unite more and more closely until, at the Synod or Ostrog,
in 1627, they became so united that from that time there has
existed in Poland no difference between the two communions.[2]

---

[1] Cf. Hutton, op. cit. p. 62; Bost, op. cit. pp. 8of., 85ff. Cranz, op. cit.
pp. 56f.
[2] Cf. Bost, op. cit. pp. 9off.; Cranz, op. cit. p. 60.

CHAPTER SIX

The Brethren in Bohemia and Moravia until their Dispersion (1548-1627)

WE must now return to trace events which took place in Bohemia and Moravia following the great emigration to Poland and Prussia in 1548. In 1558 the Emperor Charles V resigned his throne, and his brother Ferdinand I took his place. Maximilian II, the son of Ferdinand, became King of Bohemia. He was favourably inclined towards the Protestants, and those Brethren who had remained in Bohemia and Moravia began to flourish again. In 1564 they were allowed to re-open their places of worship and to hold their religious services. By 1557—just a hundred years after the first settlement at Kunwald—the Brethren were firmly established in the three provinces of Bohemia, Moravia and Poland. [1]

On hearing of the favourable turn of events in Bohemia many exiles returned home. Their enemies endeavoured to incite the Emperor to engage in fresh persecutions; in 1563 the arch-chancellor of Bohemia went to Vienna with this design. A decree was signed; but, fortunately, was not put into effect, as the arch-chancellor was drowned while returning, and the casket which contained the decree was lost.[2] The Emperor was not disposed to renew it. The Brethren were left in peace for a long period.

So much progress was made at this time that at one Synod there were present, in addition to ecclesiastics, seventeen of the most distinguished barons, and one hundred and forty-six nobles of inferior rank. At this time a desire was expressed for a new translation of the Bible into the Bohemian tongue, made from the original languages; the version which had been in use for a century was made from the Latin. In order that such an authoritative version might be made they sent some of their

[1] Cf. Hutton, op. cit. p. 67.
[2] Cf. Cranz, op. cit. p. 63.

young students to the Universities of Wittenberg and Basle that they might there learn the Hebrew and Greek tongues. This important venture was completed between 1579 and 1593, and published in six volumes. It was known as the 'Kralitz Bible.' A pocket Bible was also produced by John Blahoslaw.[1]

Already it had become a custom for noblemen and others to send their sons to study at the German Universities. It was found, however, that the benefits received were not unmixed with ill. Along with the knowledge of useful sciences they learned unprofitable things, which they introduced to their congregations, to the undermining of discipline. At the Synod of Bunzlau, in 1584, it was therefore resolved to establish seminaries of their own at three centres in Moravia. In earlier times their ministers had been prepared under the personal guidance of their own bishops and other preachers.[2]

It must be remembered that despite all this progress the Brethren were still a prescribed people. Among the papers in the royal court at Prague there was the Edict of St. James (1507),[3] which hung over their heads like a sword. Certain of the nobles now resolved to make an attempt to change this situation. When the Emperor Maximilian II died he was succeeded by Rudolph II (1576-1612) who, in 1602, under the influence of the Jesuits, confirmed the edict against the Picards (as the Waldenses and the Brethren were sometimes called). But this lasted only for a short time. Friends of the Brethren protested and it was withdrawn. And in 1609, by an imperial edict Rudolph II ratified for himself and his successors the freedom they had enjoyed under Maximilian. They were granted the privilege of erecting new churches, and choosing for themselves, out of the nobles who composed the States, patrons or advocates who should defend their rights.

Permission was also given to reform what is called 'the Under-Consistory,' which was composed of three Brethren and three Lutherans, together with three professors of the University of Prague. Moreover, the Bethlehem Church at Prague, in which Huss had preached, was restored to them. And, as it was

[1] Cf. Cranz, op. cit. p. 36; Hutton, op. cit. p. 75.
[2] Cf. Cranz, op. cit. pp. 62f.; Bost, op. cit. pp. 96f.
[3] See supra, p. 39.

Loe, here an Exile, who to serue his God,
Hath sharply tasted of proud Pashurs Rod,
Whose learning, Piety, & true worth beeing knowne
To all the world, makes all the world his owne,

JOHN AMOS COMENIUS, Painting by *Holler* from *The School of Infancy.*

not now spacious enough, they were allowed to erect another church for both Germans and Bohemians. The imperial edict was published with much joy and exultation, and the *Te Deum* was sung.[1]

In spite of this appearance of unity and prosperity, however, all was not well with the Church of the Brethren. Concerning this period Comenius, in his history of the Bohemian persecution, says: 'together with the free exercise of religion, the liberty of the flesh began gradually to appear; and good discipline was lost among those who had before strenuously maintained it.' According to Cranz, the Brethren who, on the occasion of this union, were expected to lay aside their particular church-order and discipline, had, in order to satisfy their well-wishers among other parties, made some abatement of it. To avoid the loss of their outward ease and prosperity they reckoned many points, formerly esteemed necessary, as non-essentials, and so departed from their primitive purity and strength. Consequently, they were involved in the complete overthrow of the Bohemian liberty of the Church.[2]

Immediately upon the death of the Emperor Rudolph II in 1612, the Church of Rome began to put into execution the decrees of the Council of Trent against the Protestants in general, beginning with the Bohemians and Moravians. They were subjected to all sorts of vexations and mortifications, against which the imperial edict and their own remonstrances were of no avail. By this harsh treatment they were driven to revolt, and at last, to a renunciation of their allegiance to their new King, Ferdinand II (1619-1637). They chose Frederic, the Elector Palatine, for their King. Such a revolt was just what their enemies wanted; for they could now levy war against them as rebels. It was the origin of the Thirty Years War.

At the battle of Weissenberg, near Prague, in 1620, the Protestants were defeated. Some were taken prisoners, others fled into the neighbouring countries. But soon the leading men were induced to return to their own country by an offer of pardon. On their return they were put into prison as rebels, some being condemned to perpetual imprisonment, others to death. On

---

[1] Cf. Cranz, op. cit. p. 64; Bost, op. cit. pp. 98f.
[2] Cf. Cranz, op. cit. pp. 65.

the twenty-first of June, 1621, twenty-seven of the principal lords were beheaded.[1]

Following the executions the government proceeded to carry out a systematic extermination of Protestantism throughout Bohemia and Moravia. The Anabaptists (as they were called) of Moravia, who had some forty-five colleges or districts, each containing several hundreds, and some of them a thousand, members were banished. These were more fortunate than those who remained behind. For the latter were plundered and subjected to extortions of money; and by reason of a variety of tortures and executions many fell away or quitted the country, leaving all their goods behind them. Finding that in this way the land would be stripped of its inhabitants, the rulers chose rather to banish all the Protestant *ministers*, first from Prague, and the free cities, and afterwards, in 1624, out of the whole country. Many of the expelled ministers hid themselves in mountains and caves, whence they emerged secretly to visit their congregations. Being traced out and discovered, some were put to death and others expelled the country.[2]

These violent measures were taken not only against the rebels—those who had actually taken part in the war, as was first pretended—but against all Protestants.[3] To fill the places left vacant by these proceedings many illiterate and ignorant persons, and some notoriously wicked men, were appointed as pastors. When dissatisfaction was expressed with these, a commission of reform was established to induce the Protestants who still remained in the country to recant. When it was found, however, that most of them could not be shaken from their principles, whether by force or stratagem, in 1627 all the Protestant *nobles*, after being despoiled of their goods, were banished. Hundreds of families, nobles as well as rich citizens, took refuge in the neighbouring countries, including Saxony, Silesia, Brandenberg, Poland, Prussia and Hungary; and some travelled as far as the Netherlands. The common people were strictly watched to prevent them from following their leaders. All possible means were then used to force them to apostatize;

---

[1] Ibid. p. 66; Bost, op. cit. pp. 103f.; Hutton, op. cit. pp. 83ff.
[2] Cf. Cranz, op. cit. p. 67.
[3] Ibid. p. 67; Bost, op. cit. p. 112.

or at least to practise the outward forms of the Roman Catholic religion. Bibles and other religious books were seized and burned. Some thousands of people, however, managed to escape, and certain districts were thus depopulated.

Special notice must be taken of one of the most notable men of this period, both on account of his own character and work, and because he formed a direct link between the ancient and modern history of the Church of the United Brethren.[1] John Amos, called Comenius, from Komna, the place of his birth, was born on March 28th, 1592. He studied at the Universities of Herborn and Heidelberg. In 1616 he became headmaster of the school at Przerow, which he made a kind of college. In the same year he was ordained, and two years later he was appointed minister of Fulneck, in Moravia. He had been there but three years when Bohemia had its blood-bath, as has been narrated. Fulneck was seized by the Spaniards, and his excellent library was burnt. Comenius had to flee for his life. When all the ministers were banished the country in 1624, for a short time Comenius found refuge in the mansion of a baron situated in the Bohemian mountains, whence he emerged from time to time to visit his orphaned congregation. For those in hiding he wrote his famous allegory, 'The Labyrinth of the World and the Paradise of the Heart,' which has been called the Bohemian 'Pilgrim's Progress.'

In 1627 still further action was taken against the Brethren, and Comenius, and a few other Brethren, resolved to leave Bohemia. They departed through Silesia into Poland. Even yet, however, hope was not dead. As they stood on a spur of the Giant Mountains they looked towards their homeland, and Comenius fell upon his knees and prayed that God would not quite remove His Gospel from Moravia and Bohemia, but still reserve for Himself a seed. The prayer was wonderfully fulfilled, as we shall see.

The exiles then made their way to the town of Lizza in Poland, where Comenius taught in the school. A congregation was gathered, and for a time the place became a stronghold of the Brethren. But here again misfortune overtook him; for in

---

[1] For a fuller account of his life and work, see Cranz, op. cit. pp. 68ff.; Bost, op. cit. pp. 115f.

this place he lost almost all his books in a fire, and for that, or other reasons, he left for Frankfort-on-Oder, and thence to Hamburg and finally to Amsterdam. At a Synod held at Lissa, in 1632, Comenius had been consecrated bishop of the dispersed Brethren from Bohemia and Moravia, and was the senior bishop of the Brethren, or president of the Synod, from 1648 till 1671.[1]

Comenius was recognized far and wide as one of the most learned men of his time. He was devoted to the Brethren, and by his writings, as in other ways, he rendered them great service. His writings included, *An Extract of the History of the United Brethren*, from a work written in Latin by Lusatius, a Polish gentleman of the Swiss Church; to which he added another Book, treating of the manners and institutions of the Brethren. He wrote also *An Exhortation of the Discipline and Constitution of the Church of the United Brethren;* and likewise a *Catechism*, which was printed in Amsterdam and dedicated to the Brethren, particularly to those at Fulneck and its neighbourhood.[2]

Comenius also acquired much fame as an educator and published his ideas in many books. One of these was entitled 'The Gate of Languages Unlocked'; it was translated into fifteen languages. He dreamed of the establishment of a Great Universal College which would teach all branches of knowledge. He was invited by leading men in France, Holland and Sweden to visit their countries and to expound his ideas. By the invitation of our Parliament he came to England. The outbreak of the Civil War in 1641, however, put an end to such projects.

In view of the dispersed condition of the United Brethren Comenius was deeply concerned about the preservation of their religious worship, and the continuation of a valid ministry among them; to this end, he felt, a succession of properly authorized pastors was a matter of first importance. His concern was shared by his sole colleague, John Buettner, who wrote to him on the subject, expressing a fear lest, after the decease of them both, the order of bishops, which had continued for two hundred years, should cease. Some difficulty was felt in the

[1] Cf. Cranz, op. cit. pp. 69f.; Hutton, op. cit. pp. 93ff.
[2] Cf Bost, op. cit. pp. 116ff.

selection of persons properly qualified for the purpose. At
length, the choice fell on Nicolas Gertichius, court chaplain to
the duke of Liegniz, for the congregations in Poland, and upon
Petrus Figulus, surnamed Jablonsky, from Jablonne or Gabel,
in Bohemia, for the Brethren dispersed throughout Bohemia
and Moravia. As a child Jablonsky had emigrated with
Comenius and was now his son-in-law. These Brethren were
consecrated bishops at the Synod of Mielenczyn in 1662.[1]

As Comenius, on account of his advanced age, could not
appear in person, he sent Daniel Vetter, his co-elder, to act for
him, giving him full power of consecrating in writing; which
is said to have been the custom of the primitive Church when,
in times of trouble, two or more bishops were unable to meet
to consecrate a new bishop. Peter Jablonsky, who was intended
to be the successor of Comenius for the Bohemian Church, died
before him in 1670. In the same year his son, Daniel Ernest
Jablonsky, was chosen to succeed him, and appointed to preside over the Brethren in Poland, as well as over those of the
dispersion elsewhere. It is through this same Daniel Jablonsky
that the Brethren claim that their succession of bishops was
transmitted to the Reconstituted Church when, at Berlin, in
1735, assisted by Christian Sitkovius, bishop of the Polish Brethren, David Nitschmann was consecrated bishop. Further reference will be made to this incident later.[2]

Not much definite information can be given concerning the
Brethren in the years following the dispersion of 1624-1627.
While the Thirty Years War lasted they appear to have entertained hopes of regaining the free exercise of their religion. At
the Peace of Westphalia, however, in 1648, they gained no ad-
vantage; they were left to endure the wrath of Austria. A considerable number succeeded in making their escape. Many
went to Silesia; others retired to Poland and Prussia. The greatest part went to Saxony and Upper Lusatia, where they became
inter-mingled with the rest of the inhabitants. It is calculated

[1] Cf. Cranz, op. cit. pp. 75f.; Bost, op. cit. pp. 119f.; Hutton, op. cit. p.
102.
    [2] Cf. infra, p. 88f.; The succession of Bohemian, Moravian and Polish
bishops is given by Cranz, op. cit. pp. 77ff.

that some 80,000 Bohemian subjects left their country in the years following 1624.[1]

Some of these dispersed Brethren formed particular congregations and even established new villages. Cranz gives a list of such congregations or communities from an old *History of the Bohemian Church* found in manuscript.[2] In some countries they were not allowed to do this. Sometimes they were not concerned to do it, since they hoped at sometime to return to their own country. It is scarcely surprising therefore that in some parts the Bohemian Brethren were lost sight of, and that even they themselves no longer recognized their descent. In some cases, however, this was still indicated by their names, and by definite traditions that their parents and grandparents had left Bohemia for the sake of the Gospel. This, Cranz says, was particularly the case in Upper Lusatia and in Silesia, where, about the time the awakening began in Moravia, a large number, whose descent had been lost sight of among the Germans, joined themselves to the rest of the Moravian Brethren.

Of the Protestants who stayed behind in Bohemia, some voluntarily accepted the teachings of their enemies; others conformed outwardly to the ceremonies of the Roman Church, though against their consciences, from fear of imprisonment and death. Still others hid their Bibles and other Protestant books and read them when they had opportunity in secret.[3]

---

[1] Cf. Cranz, op. cit. p. 82; Bost, op. cit. p. 120.
[2] Cf. op. cit. pp. 83f.
[3] Ibid. pp. 86f.; Bost, op. cit. pp. 124f.

CHAPTER SEVEN

Events Leading to the Reconstitution of the Church of the Brethren

IN the preceding chapter it has been shown how, after the defeat of the Protestants at the battle of Weissenberg, near Prague, in 1620, the situation of the United Brethren grew worse and worse. By the execution of the nobles, the exile of the ministers, and by the harshest measures of suppression of the people generally, the church-life of the Brethren was almost destroyed. In Bohemia and Moravia their church buildings were either destroyed or, more frequently, 'cleansed' and re-consecrated for use by the Roman Catholics. Many thousands were dispersed among different peoples, where they had little opportunity of cultivating a communal religious life. There is also reason to believe that in these distressing conditions the faith of many failed, and of others the love of Gospel-teaching became cold. This seemed to be particularly the case after the death of Comenius in 1670, and during the early years of the eighteenth century. Roughly speaking, the condition of things indicated lasted for about a century (1627-1720).

Here, however, as has so often been the case in the history of the Church, the appearances of things were deceptive. We have observed that when Comenius and his little band went into exile, he prayed that 'a seed' might be preserved in Bohemia and Moravia. We are now to note how the seed of Gospel truth, preserved and cultivated in all sorts of places, sprang into a vigorous life, and that within a few years the missionaries of the Brethren's Church were carrying the Gospel to many parts of the world.

The story is one of the most remarkable in the long history of the Christian Church.

In the year 1715 a great revival of religion began at Fulneck in Moravia, the scene of the ministry of Comenius, and also at Lititz, in Bohemia. Events in these two districts appear to have been quite independent of each other. Both districts were principal seats of the Church of the United Brethren.[1] In this work we shall confine our attention chiefly to the happenings in Moravia, since it was these which led to a reconstitution of the Church of the United Brethren. There is good reason to believe that in the neighbourhood of Fulneck, as, indeed, in many other places, there were many who secretly cherished the beliefs which had been handed down from their fathers. They read their Bibles and various religious publications, including their hymn-books. They maintained family worship; secretly held other meetings for religious fellowship; and partook of the Lord's Supper. From time to time they were examined, discovered and punished.

After the expulsion of Comenius, some of the Brethren's preachers fled to Zauchtenthal, near Fulneck, where was the last chapel to be taken away from them. Among those who held meetings here was Martin Schneider, whom the historians of the time refer to as 'the Patriarch.' He was discovered, summoned before the magistrates, and several times imprisoned. After his death the meetings were held in the house of his cousin, Samuel Schneider, who only escaped martyrdom by a miracle, and who continued to preach until his death in 1710.[2] Another stalwart of this period was George Joeschkle, of Schlen, who maintained an intimate correspondence with the Brethren in Fulneck and its neighbourhood. He was particularly concerned about his nephews, five brothers of the name of Neisser. He taught them the way of salvation, and urged them to read the Scriptures and the writings of the Brethren. Before his death in 1707 he confided his son to their care, and assured them that they would yet all see a great deliverance. The brothers Neisser were destined to play a significant part in the history of the Brethren in the days which lay ahead; as also were the Nitschmanns, their neighbours. These, and a number of others, often met together for mutual edification.

An old discharged Protestant soldier from Silesia, who appears to have been a beggar, used also to visit these meetings; and in the year 1715 he brought with him several books for

[1] Cf. Cranz, op. cit. p. 92; Bost, op. cit. p. 157.
[2] Cf. Bost, op. cit. p. 158.

the Brethren to read. He also introduced them to a number of
Lutheran ministers connected with a tolerated Protestant
Church at Teschen, which they frequently attended.[1]

The most outstanding man of this time, however, was Christian David, who appears to have been a remarkable personality
from all points of view.[2] He was born at Senftleben in Moravia
on December 31, 1690. He was educated as a Roman Catholic;
and for a time he was very zealously devoted to the practices
of that religion. For a time he worked on a farm, but afterwards learned the trade of a carpenter in a place where he
became acquainted with some evangelical Christians, who
taught him that Roman Catholic ceremonies were human in-
ventions. Soon afterwards, when these pious Christians were
apprehended and imprisoned in a cellar, Christian David used
to go and hear them praying night and day and was deeply impressed. He had not yet seen a Bible; but soon he obtained one
and read it with avidity. From that time it became his favourite
book. He became so familiar with it that even his ordinary conversation, it is said, was strangely influenced by its language.

Christian David resolved to join the Lutherans and went to
Hungary for this purpose. But when he made application the
Lutherans were afraid of incurring the penalties threatened
against those who received proselytes from popery. They advised him to go to Saxony. After visiting several places, including Berlin, he at last went to Goerlitz, where he worked as a
carpenter, and was powerfully affected by the sermons and
conversation of the Lutheran pastor, Rev. Mr. Schoeffer, and
also by the preaching of the Rev. Mr. Schwedler, of Niederwiese, near by. Here he married; and, having become deeply
concerned for the salvation of souls, he went about preaching
the Gospel.

In the course of his travels he visited Schlen, where he became acquainted with the Neissers. He conversed with them
about heart-religion, and showed them how to read the Bible
for spiritual profit. They conferred with him on their many
hindrances, and urged him to find them an asylum in a Pro-

[1] Cf. Bost, op. cit. pp. 161f.; Cranz op. cit. pp. 93f.
[2] See the longer account of him given by Cranz, op. cit. pp. 96ff.; and
by Bost, op. cit. pp. 62ff.

testant country. For many months Christian David sought for such a place without success. In the meantime they attended the church at Teschen; and in 1720 they became more intimately acquainted with its pastor, John Adam Steinmetz, a strong evangelical. He sought to dissuade the Neissers from emigrating.

Soon things took a more favourable turn. On the morning of Whit-Sunday, 1722, Christian David paid the Neissers another visit. He came to relate how, through the Rev. Mr. Schoeffer at Goerlitz, and the student John Andrew Rothe, at that time a private tutor to Baron de Schweinitz of Leube, he had made the acquaintance of Nicholas Lewis, count of Zinzendorf and Potterdorf. Not only was the count a Christian himself; he was also deeply concerned to bring others to Jesus. He had recently bought an estate in Upper Lusatia, in the neighbourhood of his grandmother, countess of Gersdorf, of Great Hennersdorf, by whom he had been educated. There he had appointed, or was about to appoint, a faithful pastor, with whom he intended to labour for the salvation of the souls of the people. In this place, Christian David said, they might find the asylum which they had so long desired.

No sooner had the Neissers heard the glad news than two of the brothers, Augustin and James, decided to leave everything and seek the new abode. Christian David had arrived on a Sunday; on the Wednesday following they resolved to quit the country. If God blessed the enterprise, the other brothers were to follow after. It was no light thing which they contemplated. It would mean leaving house and other property and many friends. All had to be done in secret. Michael Joeschke, the son of the George Joeschke already mentioned, was to travel with them.

About 10 p.m., on the Wednesday after Whit-Sunday, 1722, they began their journey. The company consisted of the two Neissers, Augustin and James, their wives and four children; their cousin Michael Joeschke, and Martha Neisser, niece of Augustin. They travelled by cross-roads and over mountains to avoid observation. The journey was rough and difficult, but they suffered no molestation, and arrived at Goerlitz, after calling at Mr. Schwedler's, the pastor of Niederwiese, in Silesia,

At Goerlitz they were hospitably entertained for several days by pastor Schoeffer. Leaving their families there, Christian David and the two Neissers, along with a citizen of Goerlitz, went on to Great Hennersdorf, the residence of countess Gersdorf, the grandmother of the count, whose protection they were seeking. They carried a letter of commendation written by the student, afterwards pastor, Rothe, to Mr. Marche, a tutor in the family. At first the countess treated them with some coldness, having been imposed upon by deceivers. But Mr. Marche interceded on their behalf, and it was agreed that they should be sent on to Bertholdsdorf, a village two miles away, of which the count was the proprietor. Mr. Rothe, who had been nominated pastor of the place, but was not yet ordained, gave them a letter of recommendation to Mr. Heitz, steward of the count's household. Mr. Heitz mentioned their arrival to the count, who was then at Dresden, where he had an administrative post.[1]

Mr. Heitz consulted with lady Gersdorf at Hennersdorf, and it was decided that it would be advisable for the party to settle upon some spot by themselves rather than in the village. With a view to their support, he proposed to them the district near the Hutberg, on the high road to Zittau. When they objected that there was no water there, he replied, 'God is able to help.' The place was marshy and covered with bushes. After the Moravians had fetched their families, lady Gersdorf sent them a cow, in order that they might be furnished with milk for the children, and ordered Mr. Heitz to show them the trees that were to be cut down for the building. Having accepted the site, Christian David struck his carpenter's axe into a tree on the spot whilst uttering the words: 'Here hath the sparrow found an house, and the swallow a nest for herself; even thine altars, O Lord of hosts.'

On the 17th of June, 1722, the three Moravians felled the first trees for the first house in Herrnhut.[2] In a letter to the count, dated July 8th, Mr. Heitz says, 'They are now full of

---

[1] The main contents of the letter are given by Cranz, op. cit. p. 98; and by Bost, op. cit. p. 168.

[2] Cf. Bost, op. cit. p. 169, who says, "On the spot where this tree stood a stone monument has since been erected."

courage and cheerfulness, intending even before winter, to build an house for themselves, and to do all the carpenter's work for themselves, without the assistance of any other person.' On October 7th they entered the first house, and about Martinmas Mr. Heitz delivered a discourse at the dedication of it on Isaiah 62:6,7: 'I will set watchmen upon thy walls, O Jerusalem! which shall never hold their peace day nor night. . . . .' Christian David offered prayer, and the service concluded with the hymn, 'Jerusalem, God's city thou, etc.'

It is pointed out that the building of Herrnhut was done in the absence of the count, and that he scarcely had any hand in it. Although he was informed of these proceedings, and agreed to accept the exiles on his estate, he took little note of the matter till after his return from Ebersdorf, where he had married, on the 7th of September, the countess Erdmuth Dorothea Reuss. On the 21st of December, when he was conducting his lady to Hennersdorf, he noticed a house in the wood, which he did not recollect having seen before. On being informed that it belonged to the Moravian emigrants, he went in, bade them welcome, fell upon his knees and prayed. Soon afterwards he moved into his newly erected mansion-house at Bertholdsdorf.[1]

The name of 'Herrnhut' given to the settlement originated with Mr. Heitz, the master of the count's household. In giving his report to the count on the 8th of July, he said: 'God has given Mr. Marche great courage to engage in this work. May he bless it, according to his loving kindness, and grant that your Excellency may build a city on the hill, called the *Hutberg* (that is, Watch Hill) which may not only stand under the guardianship and watch of the Lord; but where even all the inhabitants may stand upon the *watch of the Lord (des Herrn Hut)* so that they may not hold their peace day nor night.' This name, however, was not current till 1724, when the minister publicly made use of the appellation *Herrnhut*.[2]

During this period a spiritual awakening was taking place at Bertholdsdorf, a village near Herrnhut, through the zealous evangelical preaching of pastor Rothe, and through meetings for edification held by Mr. Heitz and Christian David. Several

---

[1] Cf. Cranz, op. cit. p. 101; Bost, op. cit. p. 172.
[2] Cf. Cranz, op. cit. p. 101; Bost, op. cit. p. 172.

awakened souls from other places joined the Moravians. Soon
there was a company of twelve persons who desired to claim
the fulfilment of the promise of Jesus that where two or three
were gathered together, He would be in their midst. Soon they
were joined by baron Frederic de Watteville from Switzerland
who, years previously at Halle, had entered into a covenant
with the count to be the property of Jesus and to serve Him
in His kingdom both among Christians and heathens. This small
company, together with the count, pastor Schoeffer of Goerlitz, and pastor Rothe of Bertholdsdorf, bound themselves more
closely to promote the kingdom of God in their own and other
places, wherever the providence of God should give them
opportunity.[1]

It will be recalled that only two of the five brothers Neisser
had in the first instance emigrated to Moravia. The three who
remained—George, Hans and Wenzel—were arrested and required to tell what had become of their two brothers. Thereupon they were imprisoned. When they were released they
requested permission of their lords, the Jesuits of Olmuetz, to
emigrate. This was refused, and they were threatened with
being imprisoned again and put into the inquisition. They
forthwith took things into their own hands, left all their possessions, and in August 1723, with their families, to the number
of ten, followed in the steps of their two brothers. Mr. Heitz
gained permission from the count to build the necessary houses
for them.[2]

Towards Christmas of the same year Christian David set out
again for Moravia. On this journey, of some two hundred miles,
he paid visits to other places in which the ancient Brethren had
lived. The story he had to tell caused a great stir among the
people, particularly those at Zauchtenthal and Kunwald. In the
latter place, the old home of Gregory the Patriarch, there still
lived descendants of the Ancient Church. In Zauchtenthal there
were three David Nitschmanns, Melchior Zeissberger, and also
John Toeltschig (who later became a preacher in Yorkshire).
These had continued to hold meetings, in consequence of which
they had been imprisoned and threatened with galley-slavery.

[1] Cf. Cranz, op. cit. pp. 101f.
[2] Cf. Ibid, p. 103.

They were direct connecting links between the Ancient and the Reconstituted Church—the first of the 'hidden seed' which Comenius had prayed might be preserved.

The five Brethren mentioned left home in May, 1724. On leaving the village they knelt down, recommended themselves, and those left behind, to the guidance and care of God. To escape the danger of being followed they took a way over the mountains. Their first design was to have gone to Lissa in Poland; or if they could find no asylum there, to Holland, where Comenius had died. But when they reached Herrnhut on the 12th of May, they found count Zinzendorf there, and also his friend baron de Watteville. They watched the little company gathered round, and saw the count lay the foundation-stone of a new building—intended for education and other purposes. Having heard the count's discourse, and the prayer of de Watteville, they felt that this was the spot to which they had been divinely led.[1]

From this time onwards there was a steady stream of emigrants from Bohemia and Moravia, many of them under the lead of Christian David, who returned again and again for this purpose. They left their houses and their goods, made their way across the mountains, running every risk, and enduring all manner of hardships. They preferred poverty and freedom in Herrnhut to the comforts and spiritual repressions in the land of their nativity.

---

[1] Cf. Cranz, op. cit. pp. 103ff.; Hutton, op. cit. p. 124.

CHAPTER EIGHT

The Early Life and Work
of Count Zinzendorf to 1724

IN view of important developments in the Church of the United Brethren which are soon to be related, it will be convenient at this point in our narrative to give some account of the early life and work of count Zinzendorf, who was destined to play a leading part in the moulding of the life of the Church until his death in 1760.

Our account will be much abbreviated, and the reader must be referred for fuller details to the authorities already mentioned, and more particularly, to the biography written by the German pastor Spangenberg, who was closely associated with Zinzendorf for the greater part of his life.[1] After a careful study of the various sources the present writer concurs in the judgement of Spangenberg that count Zinzendorf was undoubtedly one of the most extraordinary personages that have appeared in the Church of Christ since the period of the Reformation. Though differing from John Wesley in many ways, these two famous men were one in their wholehearted devotion to the cause of Christ, and in their passion to spread the truths of evangelical religion. Their lives touched one another at various points, and the movements they led became, as we shall see, strangely intertwined. This is not surprising in view of the fact that Zinzendorf, no less than Wesley, could say, 'The World is my Parish.' Both held steadfastly to the global view of Christianity; both were tireless travellers; but whereas the greater part of the travelling of Wesley was confined to these islands, Zinzendorf, though his work centred in Germany, was the greater international traveller.

[1] Cf. Rev. August Gottlieb Spangenberg, *The Life of Nicholas Count Zinzendorf, Bishop and Ordinary of the Church of the United (or Moravian) Brethren. Trans. from the German by Samuel Jackson, Esq. With an Introductory Preface by the Rev. P. La Trobe* (London, 1838). Spangenberg's Memoir was originally published between 1772 and 1775.

Count Zinzendorf was born at Dresden on May 26th, 1700.[1] His father was one of the premier ministers at the court of Saxony, and spent his short life in a laudable manner, engaged in the important duties of his office. His mother, Charlotte Justina, baroness Gersdorf, was born in the year 1675. She was a learned and pious lady, and was the count's second wife. His father died only six weeks after the birth of his son Nicholas, leaving, besides Nicholas, a son and daughter from the first marriage. His widow then removed with her infant son to her parents' home, and four years later married a field-marshal in the Prussian army. From that time the young count saw little of his mother. Until he was ten years of age he was in the constant care of his grandmother, Catharine von Gersdorf, at Great Hennersdorf. He owed much to the fact that his guardian was a devoted, pious lady, who early instilled into his mind the precepts of the Gospel. At this time a religious revival was taking place in Germany which affected all classes. It greatly influenced life at Great Hennersdorf. Celebrated Christians, like Spener, were frequent visitors, and by their religious conversation the thoughts and sentiments of the young count were moulded from his earliest years.[2]

Zinzendorf was constitutionally delicate, and did not outgrow his weakness until his twenty-first year. He had, however, a lively mind, a quick understanding, and an extraordinary memory. His disposition was both amiable and ardent. He responded quickly to the religious influences which were brought to bear upon him. When only four or five years of age he would collect chairs together, and speak to his great friend the Saviour. At six years of age he held prayer-meetings with such friends as he could assemble. We are well aware that not a few people have shown such early religious precocity, combined with vivid imaginative powers, which have found expression in similar ways. The remarkable thing about the count was that he retained his childlike characteristics and intensely spiritual devotion till the very end of his life.

When only six years of age, the count was sent to Halle, to be educated in a college for young men of the upper ranks of

---

[1] John Wesley was born June 17th, 1703.
[2] Cf. Bost, op. cit. pp. 173ff.; Hutton, op. cit. pp. 105ff.

COUNT ZINZENDORF, from Life by *Bishop Spangenberg* 1838

society, directed by the distinguished Francke, who had established there a number of important educational institutions. During this period of his life he sought by all means in his power to bring others to Jesus. He set on foot private meetings for prayer, and was often derided for his religiosity. But he persevered; and so great was his zeal that when he left Halle, in 1716, he was able to give professor Francke a list of seven societies of this kind which had been established since 1710.[1]

Whilst at Halle he several times came into contact with famous men, some of whom were concerned with missionary work. As he listened to the stories of work done in far-off lands there sprang up a desire to share in the work of foreign missions; a desire which increased as the years passed by. It was during these early years that he founded the famous 'Order of the Mustard Seed.' The boys who belonged to it took three pledges: (1) to be kind to all men; (2) to be true to Christ; (3) to send the Gospel to the heathen. Each member wore a gold ring on which were inscribed the words, 'No man liveth unto himself' (Rom.14:7). Though the first five members were of different communions, they never spent time in disputing about the points whereon they differed. They had one subject only —the sufferings and death of Christ.[2]

Two of the first five members of the Order, Zinzendorf and Watteville, as early as 1715 met together for the purpose of devising means for the conversion of the heathen. Though they knew they could not go themselves, they trusted that the Lord would lead them to someone else who could share in the enterprise.

In later years eminent men became enrolled among the members of the society which began with the five youths. They included John Potter, the Archbishop of Canterbury; Thomas Wilson, Bishop of Sodor and Man; Cardinal Noailles, and General Oglethorpe. Here we see the small beginnings of an evangelistic life-work which grew to immense proportions. When Zinzendorf left Halle to go to the University of Wittenberg, professor Francke said, 'This youth will one day become a great light in the world.[3]

[1] Cf. Bost, op. cit. p. 176.
[2] Cf. Hutton, op. cit. pp. 109f.; Bost, op. cit. p. 177.
[3] Cf. Hutton, op. cit. p. 110.

E

It is of interest to note that this unusual absorption in the religious side of school life did not mean that his studies were neglected. At fifteen years of age he could read the Greek classics; and the year following he delivered a public oration in that language. He was so ready in composition in the Latin tongue, that if a subject were given him he was accustomed to deliver his thoughts upon it without premeditation. He wrote in this language with elegance and ease.[1] He likewise possessed considerable poetic ability. Verses flowed into his mind faster than he could write them down. In later years he wrote many hymns, some of which are much used until the present time. It was not unusual for him to produce a hymn extempore to be sung immediately at a fellowship meeting.

Zinzendorf would gladly have remained at Halle to complete his studies. One of his guardians, however, urged that he should be sent to the University, in part, in order to check his religious fervour. Accordingly he went to the University of Wittenberg in September, 1716, where he remained until 1719. For a time he was lonely and unhappy, being ridiculed for his austerity and refusal to join in worldly amusements. But, like Wesley and the members of the Holy Club at Oxford, he went steadily on his way. Occasionally he spent a whole night in prayer. For a time he fasted every Friday, and later every Sunday. His studies proceeded along the usual lines; but he had a special delight in theology. As it was hoped that he would eventually fill an important office in the State, he was urged to pay particular attention to the law. He complied with the request, and the knowledge he acquired at this time proved to be of great value in the management of the affairs of the Church in later years. The same may be said of his theological studies, which must have helped to qualify him for his duties as a preacher and as a bishop of the Church.[2]

On leaving the University, after the fashion of those days Zinzendorf was sent on the grand tour through Europe, to put the finishing touches to his education. For him, however, the grand sights had little attraction: he feared lest he should be turned aside from the path of following Christ. He much pre-

[1] Cf. Bost, op. cit. p. 179.
[2] Cf. Bost, op. cit. pp. 180f.; Hutton, op. cit. p. 110.

ferred the company of ministers, bishops and cardinals to that of gay young noblemen. He was catholic in his choice of religious fellowship, delighting to hold conference with Lutherans, Calvinists and Roman Catholics. His one concern was that a man's heart should beat true to the love of Christ.

In 1719 he visited Holland, and thence went to France, still pursuing his studies. He spent several months in Paris. We can imagine the impression he made upon the worldly people who tried in vain to corrupt his morals. A young nobleman who never went to the theatre, and who was passionately absorbed in the study of the Bible was a rarity in those days.[1]

In the spring of 1720 he returned to Germany, and paid a visit to a relation at Castell. During his stay there he fell ill of fever, and remained there much longer than he had intended. He discovered that he was in love with his cousin Theodora, daughter of the countess Castell. The idea of such a marriage was favoured by the countess. But on discovering accidentally that his young friend count Reuss was also in love with her, and that she was not disinclined to him, Zinzendorf released her from the engagement. For the occasion of the betrothal he composed a cantata, which was performed before the whole house of Castell; and he also offered up a prayer on their behalf. About two years afterwards he married countess Erdmuth Dorothea, the sister of the young count Reuss, whom he had treated in so generous a fashion. She was in all ways his devoted fellow-helper in the unusual mode of life which he eventually adopted.

Zinzendorf was now of full age and the question arose as to what calling he was to follow. Left to himself he would no doubt have entered the service of the Church. But in this matter he was opposed by the wishes and plans of his friends, who had long purposed that he should enter the service of the State. His grandmother resisted all his pleadings, and he was at last constrained to accept an important legal appointment as councillor of the King of Saxony, which obliged him to reside chiefly at Dresden.[2]

At this time he bought from his grandmother the little estate

[1] Hutton, op. cit. pp. 182f.
[2] Cf. Hutton, op. cit. pp. 114f.; Bost, op. cit. p. 183.

of Bertholdsdorf, which lay about two miles from Great Hennersdorf, where he had been brought up. There he installed his friend, John Andrew Rothe, as the village pastor. Zinzendorf was resolved to work hand-in-hand with the pastor to make Bertholdsdorf a model village. In the neighbourhood there were a few persons who were distinguished both for their rank in the world and for their piety. Soon these became banded together in a fellowship of Christian service.

In 1722 baron de Watteville, of Berne, paid a visit to Bertholdsdorf. He had been a fellow-student with Zinzendorf, and a member of one of the praying societies already mentioned. From Halle he had gone to Paris, and there he had declined from the faith and become almost an infidel. In the very different atmosphere of Bertholdsdorf he became conscious of his condition, and, for a time, fell into the deepest despondency. All the members of the family sought to comfort him, and one day the expression 'God is love' was brought so powerfully to his mind that he fell on his knees, overpowered with joy, and remained in that attitude for several hours, calling on the Lord. From this time (Jan. 21st, 1723) he was bound in ever closer fellowship with the count in the service of Christ. Two other distinguished men were closely associated with them, namely, pastor Rothe and pastor Schoeffer, of Goerlitz, to whom we have referred in the preceding chapter.[1]

The powerful preaching of pastor Rothe made a great impression upon the district round Bertholdsdorf. The mode of worship adopted was also a great attraction. The preaching was followed by a general conversation between the pastor and his hearers. There was much singing, assisted by the organist, Tobias Friedrich, a man of fine character and gifts. In the afternoon there was another assembly, for his tenants and others, in the hall of the count's house, where the count, in the presence of the pastor, repeated the substance of the morning sermon.[2] When the count was absent in Dresden, this was done by the pastor himself. Similar meetings were held by the count at his house in Dresden, both on the Lord's Day and during the week.

[1] Cf. Bost. op. cit. p. 188.
[2] Cf. Hutton, op. cit. p. 127.

A printing-press was also established at Bertholdsdorf for the sole purpose of producing and circulating all sorts of religous publications. and especially the Bible. At the same time institutions were formed for the instruction of children in the principles of Christianity. Mme de Gersdorf had left legacies for this purpose. The distinguished people mentioned above entered into a written engagement to provide one thousand five hundred rix dollars for the erection of a large building, in which they proposed to establish a school for young persons of noble families, a bookseller's shop, and a dispensary to furnish medicines for the poor at a moderate cost.[1]

[1] Cf. Bost, op. cit. pp. 193f.

CHAPTER NINE

Further Developments at Herrnhut

WE may now resume the story of the settlement of the Brethren at Herrnhut at the point reached at the end of chapter seven. Count Zinzendorf is sometimes spoken of as if he were the founder of the Church of the United Brethren. The events we have recorded, and those which we have still to relate, show how far this is from being the case. When he allowed Christian David and his fellow-exiles to settle at Herrnhut, the count had no intention of having anything further to do with them. He had granted them land, provided them with a home, and allowed them to attend his meetings. They actually did, for a time, attend the services at the Lutheran Church at Bertholdsdorf, and, as we shall see, the count was annoyed when the suggestion was first made that the Brethren should break away from the Lutheran fellowship; just as John Wesley opposed the suggestion that his followers should separate from the Church of England. Zinzendorf was himself a devoted Lutheran. But so long as the Moravians lived peaceably as ordinary citizens, and attended the parish church at Bertholdsdorf, he was willing that they should follow their own devices as God-fearing tenants.[1]

At the time of which we are now speaking, about 1724, persecution still raged in Moravia. The Brethren were required to take an oath to remain in the country, to renounce their faith, and to unite with the Roman Church. The Brethren, on their side, made every effort to escape. When they attempted to carry away goods or money they were often arrested and sent back again. Sometimes they were attacked and maltreated by robbers, who deprived them of all they possessed. Nor was it easy at this time to gain admission to the colony at Herrnhut. The leaders there were fearful that the authorities in Moravia would call them to account for granting asylum to so

[1] Cf. Hutton, op. cit. p. 128.

many refugees.[1] All newcomers were therefore brought before
the authorities and carefully examined as to the motives which
had induced them to leave their country. If it was found that
they were influenced by temporal motives, and not by conscience and love of truth, they were given a few days' rest and
a little money for the journey and sent back, with a note ask-
ing the magistrates of their country to treat them kindly. The
count even made a journey to Kremsis in Moravia to appeal to
the cardinal-bishop of Olmuetz on their behalf. He also enjoined the inhabitants of Herrnhut not to return to Moravia in
order to induce others to leave the country. Despite these injunctions, however, Christian David, and various others too,
did not cease to persuade their persecuted friends to come and
join them in their new home.[2]

In addition to the Brethren from Moravia, certain other persons, chiefly from the Lutheran Church, but others also with
Calvinist sympathies, had settled at Herrnhut. It was natural
therefore that on some doctrinal matters there should be diver-
sities of opinion. It has already been observed that until this
time the emigrants had conformed to the worship of the
Lutheran Church at Bertholdsdorf. It was now felt by some of
the Moravians that the time had come to make a change. For a
time these withdrew from the worship there.[3] Among the
leaders in this new movement were the five Brethren who have
been mentioned: and these may justly be regarded as being
largely responsible for the reconstitution of the Church of the
United Brethren. From the reports of their fathers and grand-
fathers, and from the ancient hymns of the Brethren, they
brought with them ideas of the church-constitution of the
days of their forefathers. Of this they began to speak soon after
their arrival at Herrnhut. They insisted that the salutary discipline and church order of their fathers ought to be re-estab-
lished. Considerable controversy followed; the ideas of the
emigrants were strongly opposed both by pastor Rothe and
Zinzendorf. The count had long wished the new colony to unite
with the Lutherans. The crisis which now developed induced

[1] Cf. Bost, op. cit. pp. 209ff.; Cranz, op. cit. p. 108.
[2] Cf. Bost, op. cit. pp. 212f.
[3] Cf. Cranz, op. cit. pp. 112f.

him to inquire more particularly into the history and constitution of the Ancient Church of the Brethren.[1]

As the Moravians refused to yield to his wishes Zinzendorf resolved, if possible, to affect a compromise. In March 1727 he sent a declaration against the erroneous doctrines which, as he thought, were creeping into the Church; and soon afterwards he obtained leave of absence from the government at Dresden and visited Herrnhut in person. On his arrival he persuaded pastor Rothe, who had lost the confidence of the Brethren, to leave the care of the Moravian Brethren to him. He then examined each person individually, and at public meetings he discoursed on the sole ground of salvation,—without entering into the various notions which had caused confusion and division among them. In this way, after many private interviews and public discussions, he brought them to a better frame of mind. Then, on May 12, 1727, he called them together to a meeting in the 'Great House', and after a discourse lasting three hours, he read out the 'Statutes, Injunctions and Prohibitions', in accordance with which, as he proposed, the inhabitants of Herrnhut should live. These had been drawn up by the count, pastor Rothe and Mr. Marche, the president of the court of judicature. On the 8th of July they were once more ratified, and on the 12th of August they were signed by all the inhabitants.[2]

The day of these important happenings has been generally observed annually as a Memorial Day in the Church of the United Berthren. At this time the village of Herrnhut consisted of about three hundred Brethren and Sisters, one half of whom were Moravian refugees. The first article agreed upon was that, 'Herrnhut is not to be considered as a rising town or village, so much as an establishment for the Brethren.'[3]

According to the compromise now effected the Brethren engaged to return to share in the worship of the Lutheran Church at Bertholdsdorf, and to place themselves under the pastoral care of pastor Rothe, on the condition that they should be

---

[1] Cf. Cranz, op. cit. pp. 106f.
[2] Cf. Cranz, op. cit. p. 114; Hutton, op. cit. p. 129; Spangenberg, op. cit. pp. 83f.
[3] Cf. Bost, op. cit. p. 216,

allowed to manage their own spiritual affairs as a distinct society within the Church. The next step was to establish the manner of their own private discipline. The congregation was called together on May 20, 1727, and twelve of their number, men of good repute for character and experience, were chosen as elders or pastors, to watch over the engagements into which they had entered. Those elected then proceeded to choose by Lot four of their number who were to have the general superintendence of affairs. Those chosen were: Christian David, John Nitschmann, C. Hoffman, and Melchior Nitschmann. Count Zinzendorf was appointed Superintendent or Warden, and baron de Watteville was associated with him in the office. It was their duty, among other things, to see that every brother occupied his proper place in the Church according to his gifts; for many officers were appointed at this time, such as, helpers, overseers, monitors, sick-visitors and almoners. There were frequent meetings of the elders in order to consult on matters which related to the well-being of the Church. If after taking counsel together, doubts still remained on any point, appeal was made to the decision of the Lot.[1]

At this period also a night-watch was established, and every inhabitant between 16-60 years of age was in turn called to discharge this duty, which was accompanied with the singing of appropriate hymns. Numerous meetings were arranged for mutual edification. At five o'clock in the morning they assembled to read portions of the Scriptures, and sometimes to engage in prayer. At half-past eight a similar service was held for sick and aged persons.[2] On the Lord's Day, morning and afternoon services were held at Bertholdsdorf. Later an afternoon service was also held at Herrnhut, and was called 'the service for strangers.' At half-past eight or nine in the evening they assembled again in the great hall; or in winter in one of the count's apartments, for a service of song. Reports were also given of the extension of Christ's Kingdom, and prayer was offered for its success.

The larger more public meetings were supplemented by

[1] Cf. Spangenberg, op. cit. p. 84; Bost, op. cit. p. 221; Cranz, op. cit. p. 114.

[2] Cf. Cranz, op. cit. p. 123.

smaller meetings called 'bands or classes.'[1] These originated
in the desire of Zinzendorf to inquire more intimately into the
spiritual well-being of the souls committed to his care. Their
characteristic form was for two or three persons to meet together to converse on their spiritual state, and to exhort and
pray for each other. In these, and in other meetings, the two
sexes were kept apart. The members of the various bands were
often interchanged, with the result that the Brethren acquired
an intimate knowledge of each other. The Church of the United
Brethren thus became a real fellowship.

The arrangements which have been thus briefly outlined led
to a great spiritual awakening among the Brethren. On August
5th, 1727, Zinzendorf, with twelve or fourteen Brethren, spent
the whole night visiting Hennersdorf and Bertholdsdorf, and
at midnight they held a prayer-meeting on the Hutberg, which
was attended by a large number of people. On the days following, the power of God was wonderfully manifested at their
singing-meetings. There were no noisy demonstrations; but a
quiet spirit of joy pervaded the whole community. After par-
taking of Holy Communion in the parish church of Bertholdsdorf, there came to them a veritable Pentecost of spiritual
power. As they returned they agreed on a system of hourly
prayer, in which each Brother and Sister was to take turn.
Herrnhut was in very truth to be the 'Watch of the Lord.'[2]

Whilst these events were taking place, Zinzendorf found a
copy of Comenius's treatise on the constitution of the Ancient
Church. It was the 'Order and Discipline' which the last Synod
of the Ancient Church had drawn up.[3] As he read the prayer
of Comenius, that God would renew the life of the Church, he
could not but resolve then and there that: 'I, as far as I can,
will help to bring about this renewal. And though I have to
sacrifice my earthly possessions, my honours, my life, as long
as I live I will do my utmost to see to it that the little company

[1] Ibid. p. 124; Bost, op. cit. p. 223; Hutton, op. cit. p. 130.
[2] Cf. Hutton, op. cit. pp. 131f.
[3] Hutton points out that Comenius had edited the *Ratio Disciplinae*,
and Zinzendorf found the edition in the library at Zittau, a town a few
miles from Herrnhut. See op. cit. p. 131 (footnote).

of the Lord's disciples shall be preserved for Him until He comes.'[1]

The old document passed from hand to hand and was read with delight. The old laws were discovered at last. They now felt themselves to be in very truth the sons and daughters of the Bohemian Brethren.

It is to the events of this year 1727, and particularly to the 12th of May and the 12th of August, that the Brethren have generally traced the beginning of the reconstitution of their Church. In 1624 and 1627 the Church of the Brethren had been dispersed, and as far as eye could see, destroyed. Now the community at Herrnhut, consisting largely of their direct descendants, was pulsating with a vigorous spiritual life. As Cranz says, 'On the 12th of May, agreeable to the prophet Ezekiel's vision (chap.37), the dry bones having been, as it were, brought together, they were, in the following days, by various useful regulations, covered with sinews and flesh, and, on the 13th August, animated by the Spirit of the Lord; and so gradually qualified and made meet for activity, and for the service of the kingdom of God among Christians and Heathens.' Zinzendorf used to call the 12th of May 'the critical day', upon which it was decided whether Herrnhut should prove to be a nest of sects, or a living congregation of Christ.[2]

[1] Hutton, op. cit. p. 131.
[2] Cf. Cranz, op. cit. p. 118.

CHAPTER TEN

Sketch of Life at Herrnhut about 1727

I SHALL next endeavour to indicate more clearly the main features of life at Herrnhut during the period at which we have now arrived. We have seen that count Zinzendorf and baron de Watteville had been elected wardens of the community. They presided at the meetings and were generally responsible for the mode of life adopted. Under them were elders and pastors: twelve were originally chosen; and four of these were given special responsibilities for directing the affairs of the Church. The names of other officers indicate fairly clearly the duties which were allotted to them. Upon the inspectors the duty devolved of watching all occurrences in the Church and of reporting them to the monitors. The monitors, in turn, administered advice or reproof, in a spirit of love, as was thought to be necessary. Sick-visitors visited the sick every day, and saw that they were supplied with suitable medicines. The almoners inquired into the needs of the poor, helped them to find work, and, when necessary, gave them assistance from the poor-fund. As the separation of the two sexes was a fundamental principle, these duties were discharged by women among their own sex. A most important part was played by the guardians of the children.

The duties of a preacher were for some years discharged by the pastor of the Lutheran Church at Bertholdsdorf; but in the daily meetings at Herrnhut, some of the Brethren were allowed to preach when it was found that they had a sufficient knowledge of the Scriptures, and were possessed of the necessary gifts and graces.

At first the Brethren partook of the Lord's Supper every three months. But they found so much blessing in the observance of the ordinance that they expressed a desire for a more frequent Communion, and it was later arranged for them to take it every month, at first at Bertholdsdorf, later at Herrnhut. A few days before the Communion was to be held, the

elders and their assistants used to converse with each indivi-
dual; and if they found any persons in an unfit state, they
advised them to abstain for a time.[1]

Marriage and burial services were conducted by the pastor
at Bertholdsdorf. When the churchyard there became too
small a new cemetery was opened at the foot of the Hutberg.

The affairs of the Church were transacted in the conferences
of the elders. To consider and decide business of a more general nature a committee of the principal inhabitants, called the
Council of the Church, was summoned. In all doubtful cases
the Lot was used to reach a decision.

In addition to the services for Holy Communion, there were
love-feasts. At first these were of a purely private nature: they
were social gatherings of friends with a religious object. The
members partook of a little soup, cake and water: gave expression to the wish, 'Long live the Lord Jesus in our hearts'; joined
in singing His praises, and discussed how His kingdom might
be extended.

Another institution which calls for careful note was the
division of all the Brethren into ten regiments, called 'choirs'.
They were as follows: (1) the married choir; (2) the widowers;
(3) the widows; (4) the single Brethren; (5) the single sisters;
(6) the youths; (7) the big girls; (8) the little boys; (9) the little
girls; and (10) the infants in arms.[2]

Though we may well doubt the wisdom of this detailed sec-
tionalising of the life of the community, we may see in such
minute regulations an indication of the deep seriousness which
in these early days pervaded the religious and social life of the
Brethren. They regarded themselves as belonging to an army
whose captain was Jesus Christ. Thus, when the single Brethren, led by Martin Linner, bound themselves to live in one
house, they did so with the intent to be the advance guard of
the army which was to march over the world. The members
of the other choirs pledged themselves in similar ways. But the
pledges given were not made to Zinzendorf, or to any human
leader. They were made to Christ. It was He who had preserved
the seed of the Ancient Church and made it fruitful. In all

[1] Cf. Bost, op. cit. pp. 239; Cranz, op. cit. 125.
[2] Cf. Hutton, op. cit. pp. 140f. Cranz, op. cit, p. 124.

their meetings their appeal was to Him for guidance and blessing.

This was the significance of the employment of the Lot, which was used on all important occasions: for example, on the election of elders; at the undertaking of fresh missionary enterprises; and even when young people asked for advice before marriage. It was not used lightly; but only after prayer for guidance.[1]

Whilst affairs at Herrnhut were being arranged in the manner which has been briefly indicated, inquiries were received from many parts; sometimes at the rate of fifty letters a day, as to what was taking place. Rumours had spread far and wide; and many people had come to see and hear things for themselves. The count and other Brethren were invited to visit several places. This fact gave rise to deputations; for example, to Denmark (1727); to Sweden and England (1728); to Livonia (1729); to Switzerland (1730); to France (1731), and to several places in Germany.

The deputation to Denmark in 1727 was treated by prince Charles of Denmark in a most kind and gracious manner. At his own desire John and David Nitschmann brought him an account of the Brethren in Bohemia and Moravia, and of the settlement in Upper Lusatia. One consequence of this deputation, in addition to the count's personal acquaintance with the court of Denmark, was the establishment of missions among the heathen in Greenland and the West Indies. As some persons in England had desired an account of the Brethren, David Nitschmann, John Toeltschig, and Wenceslas Neisser, senior, were sent thither in 1728. A desire was expressed for a closer acquaintance with the Brethren, and the count was asked to pay a personal visit.[2]

In the summer of 1728 Zinzendorf went to Jena, with a part of his family. There he had an opportunity to give an account of affairs at Herrnhut to the students at the university, many of whom had been attending meetings arranged among themselves for mutual edification. Thence he passed to Halle, where

[1] Cf. Hutton, op. cit. p. 141.
[2] Cf. Cranz, op. cit. pp. 128ff.

he lodged in the house of Dr. Lange, and had much converse with the students.

While the count was at Jena efforts were made to induce the Brethren,—in order both to prevent a supposed persecution, and to gain more souls in those parts,—to renounce their peculiar discipline and the denomination of 'The Brethren', and to join fully with the Lutheran Church. These attempts were supported by pastor Rothe, and, strange to say, by Christian David. The count, however, despite his leaning to Lutheranism, realized the danger of the proposal, and advised them not to make any alteration until the matter had been thoroughly sifted. Even the friends at Jena, where the count then was, urged the Brethren not to be ashamed of their forefathers, but to remain in brotherly union, and to maintain the discipline which they had received by inheritance. This was done in a 'Letter of Union', which was signed by 102 Masters of Arts and students.[1]

As various defamatory reports were being spread abroad concerning the arrangements and regulations which had been made in 1727, it was thought advisable to make a more definite public statement of their designs, and of their attitude and relations to other Protestant Churches. The German and Bohemian ministers of Great Hennersdorf, the parish minister, and court of justice of Bertholdsdorf were invited on this occasion, and in their presence everything was discussed in the meeting-hall at Herrnhut with all the male inhabitants. The declarations of the Brethren were taken down in writing and delivered to the imperial notary, and solicitor to the lord lieutenant, Christian Gotthelf Marche, president of the court judicature in Bertholdsdorf. From these materials a deed was drawn up which, on the 12th of August, 1729, was signed by eighty-three men of forty-seven different families. On September 27th it was ratified by the subscription of Zinzendorf, as lord of the territory, and by Rev. Mr. Roche, as parish minister.

In this deed the Brethren first gave a narrative of the beginning of Herrnhut, declaring that they were neither separatists nor a new sect. Then followed thirteen main heads, the purport of which was to show that the Congregation of the Mora-

[1] Cf. Cranz, op. cit. pp. 132f.; Bost, op. cit. p. 263.

vian Brethren, from whom they descended, had been acknowledged by the Reformers; that they agreed with them in
doctrine; that they were not violent Hussites nor disorderly
Fratricelli; but were descended from the Brethren's Unity at
Lititz, etc.[1]

In view of the accusations that continued to be brought
against Zinzendorf, to the effect that he was founding a new
Church, and propagating strange opinions, the question was
again brought forward whether the Brethren's Church should
continue in an independent form, or unite with the Lutheran
community. There had always been present among the Brethren those who favoured the latter step; and the fact that earnest
solicitations were addressed to the count by learned men and
persons of rank were reasons for a reconsideration of the matter on January 7th, 1731.

The elders to whom Zinzendorf proposed the new project
opposed it very decidedly; but he had sufficient influence to
have it brought forward before the Council of the Congregation. The proposal was rejected by a large majority. The Brethren pointed out that their constitution was much more ancient
than that of the Protestant communions; and that for the sake
of it they, like their fathers, had left their country and their
property. Even those who were born Lutherans, and did not
belong to the Moravian Brethren, acknowledged that the constitution was agreeable to the Holy Scriptures and right reason,
and that it had been attended by many blessings. It would
therefore be wrong to depart from it.

The count, however, persisted in his attitude, and it was
decided to submit the question to decision by Lot. This, when
drawn by a child of four years of age, enjoined them, in the
language of St. Paul to 'stand fast, and hold the traditions which
ye were taught' (2 Thess. 2:15).[2] With hearts full of gratitude
the Brethren renewed their covenant with the Lord, resolving
from that time to abide by the constitution, to labour in the
work with boldness, and to preach the Gospel to all the nations.

In the year 1731 Zinzendorf visited Copenhagen, to be present at the coronation of Christian VI. He had long been highly

[1] Cf. Cranz, op. cit. p. 134.
[2] Cf. Bost, op. cit. pp. 270f.; Cranz, op. cit. p. 137.

BISHOP SPANGENBERG

esteemed at the court of Denmark, and whilst there he received the *Order of Danebrog*. The King reposed such confidence in him that he desired him to propose a worthy person for court-chaplain and professor in the university.[1]

On his return from Copenhagen the count found that above seventy new exiles had arrived from Moravia. This gave fresh occasion to his critics. He was accused of sending his emissaries to induce people to leave their homes and join the settlement. He also received an admonition from the electoral court of Saxony; to this he made a reply which seemed to give satisfaction for a time.[2]

Added force was given to the complaints made at this time by the fact that other emigrations were taking place from Bohemia. Thousands of people had left the archbishopric of Salzburg for Prussia and America.

Some of the Bohemian emigrants settled at Great Hennersdorf where they were received by Henrietta Sophia de Gersdorf, an aunt of the count, who, after the decease of his grandmother had entered into possession of the property. A revival took place under John Liberda, who was appointed assistant schoolmaster; and in four years the colony increased to four hundred persons. The lady mentioned was not well affected towards the count and his institutions, and intended to set up a kind of rival colony to Herrnhut. Dissension arose, however, between the lady de Gersdorf and the Bohemians over political and other matters. Though these things were opposed to the interest of the count, there were many who held him responsible for them.[3]

It was natural that the governments of the surrounding territories should be concerned about the movements of such considerable bodies of people from one government to another. The result was the holding of two commissions of inquiry to examine into the actual situation.

[1] Cf. Cranz, op. cit. pp. 148ff.
[2] Cf. Hutton, op. cit. pp. 144f.
[3] Cf. Cranz, op. cit. pp. 150f.

F

CHAPTER ELEVEN

The Two Commissions of Inquiry: 1732 and 1736

AFTER some less serious proceedings, which had resulted satisfactorily to Zinzendorf, the court at Saxony at length ordered an inquiry to be made into the affairs of the colony. This was welcomed by the count, and by the Brethren generally. For some time they had been in suspense, in view of the adverse reports which had been circulated. There seemed to be a possibility that upon groundless charges they might be deprived of the protection of the government without a hearing, and the whole experiment of communal life at Herrnhut be brought to an end.

It was with a sense of relief therefore that they saw the arrival of the members of the commission on January 19th, 1732. This consisted of the president of the principality of Goerlitz, baron Gersdorf of Reichenbach, to whom the examination was committed; and he was attended by the official secretary. Baron Gersdorf at once explained to the Brethren the design of the commission, which was said to be to discover whether endeavours had been made to induce the subjects of Moravia and Bohemia to leave their own countries and to join the settlement at Herrnhut; and also to inquire into their doctrine and constitution.[1]

In accordance with the instruction of Zinzendorf, during the examination the life of the community, in all its details, went on as usual. On the Sunday morning, the day after the arrival of the commission, from five to six o'clock the commissioners attended the usual daily meeting for prayer at Herrnhut. Then they went to Bertholdsdorf church, where pastor Rothe preached. They likewise attended the afternoon service, which included many visitors from the district, when again the pastor delivered a discourse. Afterwards the count delivered

[1] Cf. Cranz, op. cit. pp. 153f.

short exhortations to the various divisions of the choirs. At these meetings, and at the catechism of the children, the commissioners were present. The parish minister was afterwards interrogated by them.

On the next day the whole Congregation was assembled in the hall. After giving an address, the chief commissioner interrogated each of the Moravian emigrants, who came from about twenty different places, as to the circumstances of their awakening, the oppressions they had suffered, and their designs in coming to Herrnhut. Next the various regulations of the community were examined. On the day following inquiry was made into the institutions which had been established, including those for boys, the orphan-house, the dispensary, etc. Many questions were asked and answered.

Zinzendorf accompanied the report of the commission with a letter to the King, in which he explained the sense of the regulations of the Congregation. The Commissioners then withdrew, apparently well satisfied with the results of the inquiry. The report, however, was not issued for some months.[1]

Though the report, when eventually issued, was quite favourable, affirming the orthodoxy of the Brethren, they were in some measure involved in the dissatisfaction felt with regard to the Bohemian emigrations to which reference has been made above. By a royal edict, issued in 1732, the count was directed to sell his estates. He complied with the edict by transferring all his property to his wife. At the same time he resigned his civil offices in Dresden, in order to be able to give himself wholly to the care of the Church. He saw in the order to sell his estates the first step towards an edict of banishment.[2] About the same time he agreed, after being repeatedly urged, to resume the office of Warden of the community, which he had resigned in 1730. He then set out upon a visit to Tubingen, intending to give the professors at the university a full account of the doctrine and constitution of Herrnhut.[3]

Other developments now took place in the community. An

[1] Cf. Cranz, op. cit. pp. 155f.; Bost, op. cit. p. 312.
[2] Cf. Spangenberg, op. cit. p. 162; Bost, op. cit. p. 313; Cranz, op. cit. p 160.
[3] Cf. Cranz, op. cit. pp. 168f.

important fact was the arrival of the Lutheran minister, Augustus Gottlieb Spangenberg, a learned and pious man, who afterwards wrote the life of Zinzendorf, and in various other ways rendered great service to the Brethren. He had been assistant professor of divinity, and inspector of the orphan-house, at Halle. Differences arose between him and the authorities there, and he left to join the community at Herrnhut, where he was gladly received, and chosen to be Zinzendorf's assistant.[1]

Further, towards the end of 1732 the Church at Herrnhut expressed a desire to have a separate pastor, urging, among other reasons, that the settlement now contained five hundred souls: that the aged and infirm persons could not attend the church at Bertholdsdorf; and that they could not expect the pastor at that place to go every Lord's Day, winter and summer, to hold the meeting for strangers, etc. A memorial was presented to the magistrates, requesting that a minister should therefore be appointed as assistant to the pastor at Bertholdsdorf. They proposed a young minister from Tubingen, of the name of Steinoffer, a lecturer at the university. Pastor Rothe gave his consent to the proposed arrangement.[2]

Before Mr. Steinoffer would agree to the appointment he asked for guidance from the theological faculty of Tubingen as to 'whether the congregation of Moravian Brethren, on supposition of their agreement with the evangelical doctrine, might, and ought, abide by the regulations and well-known Church-discipline which they had maintained for these three hundred years; and yet preserve their connexion with the Lutheran Church?' The answer given was entirely favourable.

An attempt, however, was made to enforce certain conditions in this connection which were not acceptable either to pastor Rothe or to Mr. Steinoffer, and the latter accepted another appointment. Upon this, with the permission of the Elector, they sent for two ministers from Wurtemberg, to take charge of the Church in the way proposed.

In the meantime Herrnhut passed into the hands of a new sovereign of the country. On Zinzendorf's intimation to him that he had transferred his estates to his lady, in accordance

---

[1] Cf. Bost, op. cit. p. 313; Hutton, op. cit. p. 145.
[2] Cf. Cranz, op. cit. pp. 169f.

with the order made, permission was given him, and the Moravian exiles, to abide in his dominions so long as they demeaned themselves quietly and peacefully.[1]

The Church, however, perceived that the terms of the edict of toleration now granted furnished their enemies with continual opportunities of annoying them. In addition to this, the authorities of Upper Lusatia were forbidden to receive any more refugees. These considerations led them to the decision that it would be better for them not to remain together in one place, but to form different colonies, in countries where they might be allowed to sojourn, without exciting uneasiness in the governments concerned. They therefore divided themselves into two bodies. The one was composed chiefly of inhabitants of the country and of the Lutherans, who were disposed to remain at Herrnhut; the other consisted of the descendants of the Moravian Brethren, who wished to preserve their religious rights and privileges, and were prepared to form colonies, or establishments of their own, in Christian countries, and missions of the same kind among the heathen. By this means they hoped to provide for themselves, and for other Brethren who might be disposed to leave Moravia, a settled residence, and at the same time find opportunities for usefulness in heathen lands.[2]

We have seen that Zinzendorf had long been desirous of entering the ministry of the Church. After serious deliberation, and conference with the Church, he now took steps to seek the fulfilment of his wishes. There was no need for him to go through a course of study—we have already observed his deep interest in theological studies. All that was necessary was for him to present himself to some theological faculty in order to pass an examination. Several things led him to fix on Stralsund. A rich merchant of that place had asked the Brethren for a teacher—they had already supplied many such; and the count, concealing his real name, offered himself for the purpose. He took the name of M. de Freydek, which was one of the titles of the counts of Zinzendorf. Eventually he made himself known to the professors of the university. Several confer-

[1] Cf. Ibid. p. 170; Bost, op. cit. pp. 314f.
[2] Cf. Cranz, op. cit. pp. 173f.; Bost, op. cit. p. 316.

ences followed, at the close of which the count resigned his sword into the hands of the superintendent, making the promise never to wear it again, and to engage only in the work of the Lord. He set out on his return to Herrnhut on the 29th of April, 1734. He forthwith notified the step he had taken to the Queen of Denmark, and also to doctor Loescher, the Lutheran superintendent at Dresden; but he did not make it public until November.[1] His ordination at Tubingen followed soon after.

As an ordained clergyman of the Lutheran Church Zinzendorf was now fully qualified to discharge all ministerial duties belonging to such a person. In this way the critics who had objected to his preaching and his discharge of other ministerial functions were silenced.

The interest of the Brethren in foreign missions now found increasing expression. Their missionary work had begun earlier. Missionaries were sent to the West Indies in 1732, and to Greenland in 1733.[2] In 1734 a company of missionaries directed their course towards Georgia in North America. Zinzendorf had already entered into correspondence with the managers of the colony there, who now offered him a piece of land for the use of the Brethren. Hoping that they would there come into contact with the Indians, the Brethren resolved to undertake the mission. The first company set out in November, 1734. Spangenberg, who had already communicated with General Oglethorpe, the governor of the colony, met them in London and journeyed with them. They arrived at their destination in the spring of 1735. Spangenberg remained there for some years.

In the autumn of 1735 the mission was reinforced by other Brethren under the leadership of David Nitschmann. John Wesley, accompanied by his brother Charles, Benjamin Ingham and Charles Delamotte, bound for the same destination, travelled in the same ship. Of the relationship between the Methodists and the Moravians we shall speak later.[3]

---

[1] Cf. Cranz, op. cit. pp. 174f.; Bost, op. cit. pp. 319f.; Spangenberg, op. cit. pp. 177f.

[2] Cf. Hutton, op. cit. pp. 150f., 154.

[3] Cf. Cranz, op. cit. pp. 194; and see *infra*, pp. 98ff.

In 1735 three Brethren were also sent to begin work among the Swedish Laplanders.[1]

This enthusiastic missionary activity, which henceforth remained a dominant feature of Moravian church life, led to an important development in the life of the Church. The question arose whether they ought not to restore the ancient episcopal order of their own Church, so that they might be able to have ordained ministers of their own. It seemed unsafe to depend upon a succession of properly qualified Lutheran ministers to initiate and to man the missions which they felt called upon to undertake. They felt that they needed ordinations which the most rigid Episcopalians in the English colonies must acknowledge, in order that the administration of baptism and Holy Communion, and other ecclesiastical functions might be deemed valid. It was urged that the episcopal ordination of the Ancient Church of the United Brethren had been recognized by the heads of the Church of England. This had become extinct in the last Bohemian-Moravian bishop Comenius, and now existed only in the Polish branch of the Unity of the Brethren.[2]

Until this time Zinzendorf had discountenanced the proposed step for a number of reasons. For one thing, he was apprehensive lest it should furnish the occasion for an attempt to exclude the Brethren from the fellowship of the Protestant Church. He had preferred that the Unity of the Brethren should be considered as a 'Church within a Church.' But as he now considered a supply of candidates for the ministry to be an important matter he complied with the desire of the Moravian Brethren to have the episcopal ordination and church privileges of their fathers renewed. The choice fell upon David Nitschmann, who was one of those who had begun the mission in St. Thomas in the West Indies. He had also conducted a reinforcement to the colony in Georgia, and was now about to set out upon a visitation in the colonies and various missions.

Zinzendorf had already carried on a correspondence with Dr. Jablonsky, then the eldest bishop or elder of the Brethren's Unity, about the renewal of the episcopal ordination. David Nitschmann had likewise visited him several times, and was

[1] Ibid. p. 183.
[2] Ibid. p. 196, and footnote; cf. Bost, op. cit. p. 324.

examined and approved by him. He was therefore presented by the count, as the Warden of the Brethren, to Jablonsky, in a letter dated 6th March, 1735, and by him, with the concurrence of his colleague Sitkovius of Lissa in Poland, and in the presence of some witnesses of the Bohemian nation, consecrated a bishop. on March 13th at Berlin, of the Congregations of the Moravian Brethren.[1]

In 1736 Zinzendorf seems to have had a presentiment that he might again be sent into exile. For during this year he held numerous conferences with the elders of the community, and conversed intimately with all its members, inquiring closely into the condition of all the institutions. For one thing, the King of Denmark appeared to have taken an unfavourable view of his new profession. Zinzendorf had written to ask either his positive consent to his becoming a clergyman, or his permission to send back the Order of Danebrog, which he had kept till this time. The King replied that he could not approve of his ecclesiastical profession, and he had only to return his Order, which he did.[2]

About this time the count was invited by the princess of Orange to visit her at Lewarden, in order that she might converse with him on a project she had conceived of founding a colony of the Brethren at Ysselstein in Holland. Before setting out the count visited Herrnhut, under the impression that he would be exiled before he could visit the place again. When he arrived in Amsterdam he hired a house for himself and the two Brethren who accompanied him, and established there the same style of life as at Herrnhut.

We may here anticipate a little and say that as a result of this visit, in the beginning of 1737 a colony was established to which the name of Hoerendyk was given, and was chiefly intended as a resting-place for missionaries going to and from their stations. It was later removed to Zeist.[3]

On April 6th, 1736 Zinzendorf left for Cassell. On his arrival he found awaiting him a copy of the King's order to him to leave the country. Shortly afterwards he met David Nitsch-

[1] Cf. Cranz, op. cit. p. 197; Bost, op. cit. p. 325.
[2] Cf. Bost, op. cit. p. 328.
[3] Cf. Cranz, op. cit. p. 202; Bost, op. cit. p. 330.

mann, who had come from Herrnhut to bring him the original order. Nitschmann also informed him that a commission was going to Herrnhut to bring the colony to an end. On receiving the order the count, in no way disturbed, said: 'the moment is come for collecting together a Church of pilgrims; we must go and preach the Saviour of the world.'[1]

Following out this idea Zinzendorf gathered together such of the Brethren as were being prepared for active service in the cause of God, and resolved to employ himself in fitting them for their work. They were occasionally joined by missionaries returning from their stations abroad, and by those who had been sent as deputations to various parts of Christendom. In this way was constituted the 'Church of the Pilgrims', a kind of missionary Congregation, changing station whenever the count changed his residence, but, at the same time, strictly observing all the regulations which had been established at Herrnhut.

Though himself in exile, Zinzendorf judged it right to send back the countess to Herrnhut, that she might be there during the sitting of the commission. He agreed with her that she might make use of all her fortune in the support of her household, without sending him the least contribution: he would endeavour to support himself and his pilgrims. Already, through his various establishments, he had incurred heavy debts. Providentially, as it seemed, a rich man in Holland, who was scarcely known to the count, offered to discharge all his debts, receiving a moderate rate of interest on the sum advanced.

Every member of this wandering Church, who had any fortune, provided for his own wants: he who had nothing was supported by the rest. As in the case of any nobleman's house, there were numerous servants of both sexes; but no one was paid for services rendered.

This second commission consisted of four important officials, led by the deputy-lieutenant of Upper Lusatia. It arrived on the 9th of May, 1736, and continued till the 18th. Now, as on the former occasion, the Brethren continued their usual routine of meetings, etc. The inquiries made were even more rigorous

[1] Cf. Bost, op. cit. p. 331; Spangenberg, op. cit. p. 206f.

than before. The Commissioners expressed their satisfaction with the doctrine taught; but suggested certain changes in the constitution. The Brethren, however, feeling that any change now made would be misconstrued, declined to make any concessions, offering to emigrate rather than do so. The suggested changes were therefore not pressed.

All the commissioners, and Dr. Loescher, the superintendent of Dresden, in particular, acknowledged the count's innocence, extolled the good order of the Congregation at Herrnhut, and exhorted the Brethren to continue on the good foundation of the doctrine they had expressed, and to persevere in their union with the Lutheran Church. This, however, was only the opinion of the commissioners; for the royal decision they had to wait fifteen months. It was not received until the third commission was appointed, in the month of February 1737. This had reference to all the Bohemian emigrations to the States of Upper Lusatia. The Brethren were once more acquitted of blame. The royal decree was to this effect: 'That the congregation of Herrnhut shall, as long as they continue in the doctrine of the unaltered Confession of Augsburg, be left undisturbed in the regulations and discipline, as hitherto.'[1]

---

[1] Cf. Cranz, op. cit. pp. 205f.; Bost, op. cit. pp. 335f.

CHAPTER TWELVE

The Brethren at
Ronneberg and Marienborn

IN the month of June 1736 count Zinzendorf went to Ebers-dorf in Vogtland, the home of his brother-in-law, count Henry Reuss. After holding a conference with some of his fellow-labourers, whom he had invited to meet him there, he went to Wetteravia. In that district, situated about thirty miles N. East of Frankfurt-on-Main, there were two old ruined castles called Ronneberg and Marienborn. The owners of the estates, the counts of Isenberg, had got into debt, and their estates were falling into ruin. The out-buildings and the farms had been let out to people of the lowest classes. When the counts heard of Zinzendorf's banishment from Saxony they offered him the lease of the estates. Zinzendorf sent Christian David to examine the situation; and despite the adverse report he gave of the property and its situation, Zinzendorf decided to make the district the centre of his work.[1]

For a time the count chose for his abode the old ruinous castle of Ronneberg, largely because in its environs there lived many poor and ignorant people to whom he wished to mini-ster. He arrived there on June 14th, 1736. On the Sunday fol-lowing he preached on 'The Lost Sheep.' The service was attended by Christians of various persuasions, and even by Jews. He set up schools for the children, and distributed food and clothing among them. To this place his wife followed him in July, with their children. She had remained at Herrnhut till the commission had completed its work, and had also made careful provision for the management of the institutions there. Here also those Brethren met who were intended to undertake missionary work in various parts of the world.[2]

On July 27th, Zinzendorf set out upon a journey to Livonia,

[1] Cf. Spangenberg, op. cit. p. 213; Hutton, op. cit. pp. 165ff.
[2] Cf. Cranz, op. cit. p. 208; Bost, op. cit. pp. 336f.

a country which he had long wished to visit, and travelled by way of Jena, Halle and Berlin. Christian David and David Nitschmann had already visited this district, and many persons of rank, both of the laity and clergy, had expressed a wish for the count to visit them. During the visit he had fruitful conversations with many influential people.

On his return through Berlin he was invited to wait upon Frederick William I, the King of Prussia, who, on account of rumours and ill-reports, had been greatly prejudiced against him. During three days he had long conversations with the King who, at the close of them, stated in the presence of the whole court, that he regarded the charges brought against the count of disturbing the Church and the State as altogether calumnious. He also added that while Zinzendorf's plan of labouring in the work of God, in his character of a nobleman, was singular, there was nothing blameworthy in it. It was to be approved rather than condemned.[1]

The King also advised Zinzendorf, in order to regularize matters, and thus to avoid giving offence, to seek ordination as a bishop. The advice strengthened an inclination he had himself long felt. For the sake of the Moravian Brethren the ordination of the Church of the United Brethren was required; and no one could confer this upon him except the eldest bishop of the Unity, Dr. Daniel Ernest Jablonsky, who at that time was the dean of the King's Chapel at the court of Berlin, and David Nitschmann. The King therefore ordered the dean of his chapel to confer with the count on this matter. Upon the report which Jablonsky made of the result of the conference, the count requested the King, as a condition without which he could not receive ordination, that the Lutheran deans at Berlin might first examine him as to orthodoxy; as he did not wish to enter the office except as a Lutheran divine. The King having agreed to this, the count laid all the proper documents before the deans, and allowed them six months to examine them. He then resumed his journey to Wetteravia.[2]

Before he reached Ronneberg, however, he learned that his wife and family, together with the Brethren who were with

---

[1] Ibid. op. cit. p. 211; Bost, op. cit. p. 338; Spangenberg, op. cit. p. 220.
[2] Cf. Cranz, op. cit. pp. 211f.; Hutton, op. cit. p. 170.

her, had been driven out of the place by the ill-will of the
steward (who would not allow the preaching of the Gospel
and the work of the charity school) and had gone to Frankfurt; and to that place he went to join them. Before setting
out on a journey to England he held, in Marienborn, with the
consent of the count of Meerholz, the first Synod of the Reconstituted Church of the Brethren. It lasted from the 10th to the
12th of December 1736. The Synod consisted of such labourers
from Herrnhut and other places, as happened to be there with
him.[1] The castle was afterwards rented as the abode of the
Brethren. This was just fourteen years after Christian David
had felled the first tree at Herrnhut. For another fourteen years
the ruinous old castle was to be the home of the Moravian
Brethren, whom Zinzendorf called the 'Warrior Band.' It was
the headquarters of a body of Christians who were called to
"proclaim the Saviour of the World."

At Marienborn all the members lived together in the castle.
The countess managed the household arrangements. Polycarp
Müller was professor of theology. Spangenberg looked after
the young men. Our modern ideas of life in a castle may easily
lead us to misconceive the situation of the Brethren at this
time. The district was wild, and the castle crumbling to pieces.
The Brethren slept on straw. There were rats and mice in
plenty. From morning till evening the Brethren were kept busy.
There was much Bible study and united prayer: languages had
to be learned; and likewise some mode of earning a living. The
latter item was important in view of the fact that when the
Brethren landed on a foreign shore they were usually practically penniless, and had to maintain themselves by the work
of their own hands.[2]

The old castle also became an evangelistic centre for the
surrounding district. The Brethren conducted free schools for
the children; held meetings for men and women in the vaults
of the castle; and provided food and clothing for those in need.
At Herrnhaag or 'Lord's Grove', near by, they shortly afterwards began to build a regular settlement on the same plan
as that at Herrnhut, with a Brethren's House and a Sisters'

[1] Ibid. p. 213.
[2] Cf. Hutton, op. cit. p. 167.

House. Gardens were laid out and fields were tilled. In a few years the members here exceeded those at Herrnhut.[1]

For some time Zinzendorf had designed to visit England. On his way thither he passed through Holland. At the Hague he had many discussions with important personages. He arrived in London on January 20th, 1737. His main desire was to confer with Dr. John Potter, who, after being Bishop of Oxford, had just been promoted to be Archbishop of Canterbury, on the question of the Moravian Church, and, particularly, on the ordination which he himself was shortly to receive. Several years previously he had written to him on this subject; though through some miscarriage the letter had not been answered.

On this occasion Zinzendorf also became acquainted with General Oglethorpe, and the trustees of Georgia, with whom he conferred concerning the colony of the Brethren at that place. Some of the trustees were associates of the late Dr. Bray, who had, by his last will and testament, made provision for the conversion of the negroes of South Carolina. These gentlemen requested the count for some missionaries to be sent there. When he objected that the Church of England would not acknowledge the Brethren as being duly ordained, they sent deputies to consult the archbishop on the matter. They received from him the following answer: 'That the Moravian Brethren were an apostolical and episcopal Church, not sustaining any doctrines repugnant to the XXXIX Articles of the Church of England; that they, therefore, could not with propriety, nor ought to, be hindered from preaching the Gospel to the Heathen.'[3]

The count returned to Germany, and after a short stay at Frankfurt-on-Main, he went with his family to Berlin. There he presented himself for the examination as to orthodoxy which he had himself requested, and which the King had directed the deans to take in hand. Their report to the King was to the effect: 'That they found no other doctrine held by

[1] Ibid. p. 168.
[2] Cf. Cranz, op. cit. p. 213; Bost, op. cit. p. 340.
[3] Ibid. p. 214.

him, but what is taught in the evangelic[1] Church.' After answering certain further questions that had been raised, Jablonsky was given the necessary rescript to carry out the ordination. On May 20th, 1737, Zinzendorf, in the quality of a Lutheran divine, received episcopal ordination at the hands of the eldest bishop of the Polish Church, and of the first bishop of the Reconstituted Moravian branch, David Nitschmann, and with the concurrence and blessing of the elder Sitkovius of Lissa. The Archbishop of Canterbury cordially congratulated him upon the event, promising his utmost assistance to this Church of confessors.[2] From this time onwards the count was commonly known as 'the ordinary of the United Brethren."

During the count's stay at Berlin his father-in-law, General de Nasmer, obtained from the King of Poland permission for him to return to Herrnhut. He arrived there on June 30th, 1737. He soon found, however, that his return was made conditional upon his signature of the deed which required him to remedy many disorderly things which were laid to his charge. This he could not do without tacitly acknowledging that he had been guilty of the said disorders. As he felt himself to be entirely guiltless of these, he requested that there should first be an examination of the charges, at the same time promising that if they were found to be substantiated he would then sign the deed. As his petition was not granted, he went for a third time into exile on December 4th, 1737. This was viewed as perverse obstinacy on his part, and on the 13th of April, 1738, a return to Saxony was forbidden him for ever. Actually, however, the exile was terminated in ten years.[3] The count went to Wetteravia and busied himself with the development of the colony at Herrnhaag, near Marienborn. He intended this to serve as a place of asylum for members of the Reformed Church, as Herrnhut did for the Lutherans.

During this year the settlements at Herrnhut and Marienborn were visited by John Wesley and his friend Benjamin Ingham, along with a few others. Of this visit we shall speak

[1] So the Lutheran Church is called at the German courts. See Cranz (footnote), p. 215.
[2] Cf. Cranz, op. cit. p. 216; Spangenberg, op. cit. p. 227
[3] Ibid. p. 216f.; Bost, op. cit. p. 342.

later. So far as the Brethren were concerned the period was one of intense missionary activity. Missionaries were sent to Guinea, the Cape of Good Hope, to various parts of South America, Ceylon and to many other places.[1]

The most important event of the year was Zinzendorf's own setting out on a visitation of certain overseas' stations. First he went to Holland, and whilst there he published an answer to a so-called 'Fatherly Pastoral Letter' against the Brethren which had been sent out by the Consistory of Reformed Ministers at Amsterdam. He then embarked for St. Thomas in the West Indies. Part of his design in going to this place was to shut the mouths of some of the Germans who had complained about his sending people into an unhealthy climate, where they must soon die, and not going himself. He arrived at his destination, along with some other Brethren and Sisters on 29th January, 1739, travelling by way of St. Eustatia.[2]

On his arrival he found that the governor of the Island, instigated by a combination of traders, planters and clergy, had thrown the missionaries into prison, where they had lain for three months. Zinzendorf at once appealed to the governor, who set them free the next day, and apologised for what had happened. For two months the count preached to the negroes. He also made representations to the Danish King, with the result that orders were given that the Brethren were to be permitted to labour among the negroes without further molestation.[3]

Zinzendorf sailed for England, returning by way of the Islands of St. Croix and St. Eustatia. Like his great contemporary, John Wesley, during his travellings the count was always incessantly engaged in writing: and during this voyage home, he composed the well-known hymn, which begins, 'Jesus, Thy blood and righteousness, my beauty are, my glorious dress.' He arrived in England on the 20th of April, 1739, and found a great revival in progress. He reached Marienborn in June, sick and emaciated, full of boils and sores.[4]

[1] Cf. Cranz, op. cit. pp. 223ff.
[2] Cf. Bost, op. cit. pp. 343, 347.
[3] Cf. Cranz, op. cit. pp. 234ff.; Hutton, op. cit. p. 171.
[4] Ibid. p. 243.

JOHN WESLEY, M.A., from a Scarce Engraving 1743 from
Tyerman's *Life and Times of John Wesley* (1870)

At Marienborn he found his son Christian Renatus. He had
returned from Jena, with his tutors and some other students
of divinity who had followed him thither. This was the beginning of the theological seminary at Herrnhaag, which soon
after received an increase from Halle, and, gradually, from
other universities, both inside and outside Germany. From this
seminary the Church of the Brethren and other Protestant
Churches were supplied with faithful ministers of the gospel.[1]

During the next few years Zinzendorf was busily engaged
in holding conferences and Synods, despatching missionaries
to east and west, and in travelling and preaching.

The temper of Zinzendorf's mind at this period finds a
worthy expression in a letter written by him to a friend about
the year 1740. He says, 'One of my favourite plans is to contribute, as much as lies in my power, to the accomplishment
of the grand design of our Lord (John xvii), the gathering
together of the children of God. I do not wish to join in the
bond of the Moravians, but in that general communion, in
which the Moravian sect must be at length lost, and this dis-
tinction become quite unnecessary for the particular work
which is now assigned them ... I have incessantly endeavoured
to unite all the children of God, even those who do not reside
in the same place. This latter plan, however, I am beginning
to abandon, not only because I see no means of accomplishing
it, but because I think I discover, in the opposite state of things,
a secret working of Divine Providence.'[2]

---

[1] Ibid. p. 244.
[2] Cf. Bost, op. cit. p. 353.

CHAPTER THIRTEEN

Methodists and Moravians

WE have already seen that in 1734 the Moravian Brethren established a mission in Georgia, North America, on a piece of land which was offered them by the managers of the colony. Spangenberg, who had been in communication with General Oglethorpe, governor of the colony, concerning this matter, travelled with the first group of missionaries and remained with them for several years. Another group of missionaries went out to strengthen the mission the following year under the leadership of David Nitschmann.[1] In the same vessel there travelled John and Charles Wesley and their friends Benjamin Ingham and Charles Delamotte. The Wesley brothers were destined to become the leaders of the greatest religious revival this country has ever known, whilst Ingham was to become one of the best known leaders of the work of the Brethren in this country. Charles Delamotte likewise became a Moravian.

From the early years of the eighteenth century the two movements were closely intertwined. How deeply indebted John Wesley, in particular, was to the personal influence, teaching and doctrine of the Moravian Brethren is well known to all students of the work of Wesley and his associates. It is fully acknowledged by Wesley's biographers, and by the historians of the Methodist movement. But not all have sufficiently recognized how ancient was the Church of the United Brethren when Wesley first came to know it, or how valiant had been its witness to the truth of the Gospel and to the reality of the Christian experience which were about to make so deep and permanent an impression upon the religious life of this country and of the whole world. As readers of our earlier chapters will have perceived, the Church of the United Brethren did not begin with count Zinzendorf. When he arrived upon the scene that Church had had a long and honourable

[1] See *supra*, p. 86.

history: it had sown the seed which had helped to prepare for the great Lutheran Reformation. Its teaching, constitution and discipline had been approved by the Reformers: it had known great leaders, whose names are worthy of a place in any record of the achievements of the Christian Church. But Zinzendorf was by far the most prominent leader of the Brethren at the time when John Wesley began his great work. Wesley was a little the younger of the two—Zinzendorf having been born in 1700, Wesley in 1703.

It was not likely that two such dominating personalities would always see eye to eye. Both were religious enthusiasts from their earliest days: though not in any objectionable sense. Both were throughout life passionately intent upon doing the work to which they felt God had called them. Yet the background of their lives, though equally religious, was different in many ways. Behind Wesley lay the puritan movement of the seventeenth century and the reaction to high churchmanship of his parents; behind Zinzendorf lay many centuries of deep devotion to Bible study and to an evangelical conception of religion which, though not unknown elsewhere, found amongst the Brethren an unusual emphasis. If we keep these facts in mind it will not seem so surprising that, as the two movements progressed, discordant elements appeared from time to time, and that the leaders and followers alike failed to appreciate both the spirit and the methods of the other side.

In this chapter we shall give a brief account of the mutual relationships of these two great movements at the period at which we have now arrived, and also give a few intimations of events which followed. Those who desire to study a fuller account of the various personalities and incidents from the Methodist point of view may be referred to the many works which deal with the life and work of Wesley, a few of which will be mentioned.

When the two Wesleys and their two friends went on board the *Simmonds*, off Gravesend on October 14th, 1735, they found twenty-six Moravians already on board, travelling under the care of their bishop David Nitschmann, of whose episcopal ordination some account has been given. Within two or three days John Wesley had begun to learn German, in order to be able to converse with his fellow-travellers. Throughout the voyage all were busily occupied in the study of the Bible, and other religious literature; in private and public prayers; in exposition and in preaching. Wesley joined the Moravians in their public service. In a letter to his mother, Ingham said of the Moravians: 'They are a good, devout, peaceable, and heavenly-minded people; and almost the only time you know they are in the ship is when they are harmoniously singing the praises of the great Creator, which they constantly do twice a day. Their example was very edifying. They are more like the primitive Christians than any Church now existing, for they retain both the faith, practice and discipline delivered by the apostles . . . "[1]

The voyage was very stormy, and the ship rocked violently. The English passengers began to scream; but the Germans calmly continued their singing. Wesley was greatly impressed by this, and, at the conclusion of their service he asked one of them: 'Were you not afraid?' He answered, 'I thank God, No.' Wesley asked again, 'But were not your women and children afraid?' 'No,' replied the Moravian, 'our women and children are not afraid to die.' With this object-lesson before him Wesley pointed out to the terrified English the difference which faith in God makes. In his account of the storm Wesley says, 'This was the most glorious day which I have hitherto seen.'[2]

The missionaries arrived in the Savannah river on February 5th, 1736. As soon as they had stepped ashore Wesley and his friends knelt down and gave thanks to God for their safety amidst the perils of the sea. The next day one of the first to greet them was the Moravian elder, August Gottlieb Spangenberg, from Savannah. Wesley sought his advice about his own work, Spangenberg replied that he could say nothing until he had asked him a few questions. The first was: 'Have you the witness within yourself? Does the Spirit of God bear witness with your spirit that you are a child of God?' Wesley was surprised by the question, and knew not what to answer. His next

[1] Cf. Tyerman, L., The Life and Times of the Rev. John Wesley, M. A. (1890). Vol. i. p. 121.
[2] Cf. Curnock, N., The Journal of the Rev. John Wesley, A.M. (1938), Vol. i. p. 143.

question was: 'Do you know Jesus Christ?' Wesley hesitated, and said, 'I know He is the Saviour of the world.' 'True,' he replied, 'but do you know He has saved you?' He answered, 'I hope He has died to save me.' He only added, 'Do you know yourself?' Wesley said, 'I do;' but he adds, 'I fear they were vain words.'[1]

Whilst Ingham and Charles Wesley went off with Oglethorpe to Frederica, Wesley and Delamotte, having no house of their own to live in, lodged for a month with Spangenberg, Nitschmann and other Moravian friends. They thus had ample opportunity to observe their way of life. Wesley says of them that, 'They were always employed, always cheerful themselves, and in good humour with one another; they had put away all anger and strife, and wrath, and bitterness and clamour and evil speaking; they walked worthy of the vocation wherewith they were called, and adorned the Gospel of the Lord in all things.'[2]

Wesley was present at the election and ordination of Anton Seifart[3] as a Bishop for Georgia. Of the proceedings, he says 'The great simplicity, as well as solemnity, of the whole, almost made me forget the seventeen hundred years between, and imagine myself in one of those assemblies where form and state were not, but Paul the tent-maker and Peter the fisherman presided, yet with the demonstration of the Spirit and of power.'[4]

So intimate did Wesley become with the Moravians in Georgia, and so strong was his confidence in their judgment, that he consulted the Moravian bishop David Nitschmann as to whether he should proceed with his marriage to Miss Sophey Hopkey, niece of the chief magistrate of Savannah. When the bishop recommended caution, Wesley resolved to submit the matter to the elders of the Moravian Church. Nitschmann asked him whether he would abide by their decision, and after some hesitation Wesley replied that he would. 'Then,' said

[1] Ibid. p. 151.
[2] Cf. Tyerman, op. cit. Vol. i. p. 126.
[3] Ibid. Vol. i., p. 126; Cf. James Hutton's Memoirs, p. 22.
[4] Cf. Curnock, op. cit. Vol. i., pp. 170f.

Nitschmann, 'we advise you to proceed no further in the matter!' Wesley answered, 'The will of the Lord be done!'[1]

Painful as the decision was, Wesley soon recognized that it was in accord with God's will for him. Referring to the fact that within a short time she married another, Wesley made the following entry in his *Journal*: 'being slack in the execution (of his resolve to give her up) . . . God being very merciful to me, my friend performed what I could not.'[2]

With the troubles which came to Wesley during the days that followed these unpleasant incidents we shall not concern ourselves. Within a short time Wesley had decided to leave the colony. On December 2nd, 1737, he took boat for Carolina, on his way to England. He landed at Deal on February 1st, 1738. His brother Charles had preceded him by fourteen months. Whitefield left England for America the day before Wesley reached it.

We have seen that during his voyage to America, and during his stay in Georgia, Wesley had become greatly indebted to the Moravians for advice and guidance. By their example, as well as by their teaching, he had been convicted of his lack of saving faith. As he himself expressed it, he had 'the faith of a servant, though not that of a son.' He was only 'almost a Christian.'[3] Under the influence of the Moravians he was now to receive a further blessing which changed the whole quality of his life and ministry.

Soon after his return to London, Wesley met, at the house of a Dutch merchant, Mr. Weinant, Peter Boehler and two friends who had just landed from Germany. When Wesley found that they had no friends in London, he secured them lodgings near Mr. Hutton's, in Westminster, where he generally stayed whilst in London. Boehler was twenty-five years old, and had studied theology at the University of Jena. Zinzendorf, who at that time resided in London, had received a request for some Brethren to work among the negroes of South Carolina, in N. America. For this mission Peter Boehler had been called from

[1] Cf. Tyerman, op. cit Vol. i. p. 147.
[2] Ibid. pp. 148f.
[3] Ibid. Vol. i. pp. 167, 176.

Jena and ordained minister of the colony of Brethren in Georgia.[1]

John and Charles Wesley requested Boehler to go with them to Oxford. Wesley talked much with him, but could not understand his teaching. He was greatly perplexed when Boehler said to him, 'My brother, my brother, that philosophy of yours must be purged away.'[2] In a letter to Zinzendorf Boehler gives his impressions of the two Wesleys at this time. He says, 'I travelled with the two brothers, John and Charles Wesley, from London to Oxford. The elder, John, is a goodnatured man: he knew he did not properly believe on the Saviour, and was willing to be taught. His brother, with whom you conversed a year ago, is at present very much distressed in his mind, but does not know how he shall begin to be acquainted with the Saviour. Our mode of believing in the Saviour is so easy to Englishmen, that they cannot reconcile themselves to it; if it were a little more artful, they would sooner find their way into it. Of faith in Jesus they have no other idea than the generality of people have. They justify themselves; and, therefore, they always take it for granted, that they believe already, and try to prove their faith by their works, and thus so plague and torment themselves that they are at heart very miserable.'[3]

Such was, indeed, the condition of the Wesleys at this time. Their faith was imperfect; at heart they were very wretched. About fourteen days afterwards Wesley met Boehler again when he visited his brother Charles, who was lying ill in Oxford. 'By him,' he records in his *Journal*, 'I was, on Sunday the 5th (March, 1738) clearly convinced of unbelief, of the want of that faith wherby alone we are saved.'[4] But when Wesley concluded that he was therefore unfit to preach, and asked Boehler, 'What can I preach?' he replied, 'Preach faith *till* you have it, and then, *because* you have it, you *will* preach faith.' The advice was followed by Wesley.

Before the end of April Wesley was convinced that Boehler's views on the nature and fruit of faith were truly scriptural.

---

[1] Cf. Cranz, op. cit. p. 226.
[2] Cf. Curnock, op. cit. Vol. i. p. 440.
[3] Cf. Tyerman, op. cit. Vol. i. pp. 181f.
[4] Cf. Curnock, op. cit. Vol. i. p. 442.

Yet he could not understand how such faith could be instantaneous; but when he read the Acts of the Apostles he found to his surprise that nearly all the conversions there recorded were instantaneous. He was then ready to conclude that such wonders were peculiar to the first ages of Christianity. But he was beaten out of this retreat too, 'by the concurrent evidence of several living witnesses who were brought to him' by Boehler. 'Here,' says Wesley, 'ended my disputing. I could now only cry out, "Lord, help Thou my unbelief".'[1] The day of his deliverance was now near at hand.

On the first of May, 1738, Wesley was recalled from Oxford on account of his brother's illness. He found Charles at the house of James Hutton, near Temple Bar. Here, on the same evening, a little Society, formed on the advice of Boehler, met for the first time. It was afterwards transferred to Fetter Lane. Two days after the Society was formed, Charles Wesley, during a long conversation with Boehler, was convinced of the nature of evangelical or saving faith. The next day Boehler embarked for Carolina. On his departure, Wesley wrote, 'Oh, what a work hath God begun since his coming into England, such an one as shall never come to an end till heaven and earth shall pass away.'[2]

On Whit-Sunday, May 21st, rather more than a fortnight after Boehler left London, Charles Wesley found joy and peace. Three days later, May 24th, John experienced the same blessing. During the afternoon he had attended a service at St. Paul's Cathedral, where the anthem sung had been, 'Out of the deep have I called unto Thee, O Lord . . . ' In the evening, he relates, he went very unwillingly to a Society in Aldersgate Street, where one was reading Luther's Preface to the Epistle to the Romans. In giving his account of the experience which followed, Wesley says: 'About a quarter before nine, while he was describing the change which God works in the heart through faith in Christ, I felt my heart strangely warmed. I felt I did trust in Christ, Christ alone for salvation; and an assurance was given me that He had taken away *my* sins, even *mine*, and saved *me* from the law of sin and death.'[3]

[1] Ibid. Vol. i. p. 455.
[2] Cf. Telford, John, *Life of Wesley*, p. 99.
[3] Cf. Curnock, op. cit. Vol. i. pp. 475.

Forthwith Wesley began to pray for those who had persecuted him, and testified openly to all present what he now felt
in his heart. Towards ten o'clock he was taken to his brother
Charles, and together they sang a hymn which Charles had
composed the day before on his own conversion.

CHAPTER FOURTEEN

John Wesley's Visit to Herrnhut

IN view of the great assistance which Wesley acknowledges to have received from the Moravians in his pursuit of a richer spiritual experience, it is not surprising that he should have conceived the idea of going to visit their headquarters at Herrnhut and elsewhere in Germany. Already he had received much information concerning the mode of life there which had greatly attracted him.[1] Accordingly, three weeks after his evangelical conversion he set out upon this journey. One of his companions was Benjamin Ingham, who had been Wesley's companion in Georgia; another was John Toeltschig, who later exercised a distinguished ministry among the Brethren in Yorkshire; and there were several others.[2]

On June 16th, 1738, they arrived at Ysselstein, in Holland, the home of baron de Watteville. Here as we have already seen, the Brethren had established a small colony or settlement.[3] Wesley and his friends spent a day with them, 'in hearing the wonderful work which God was beginning to work over all the earth, and in making our requests known to Him, and in giving thanks for the mightiness of His kingdom.'[4] Proceeding *via* Amsterdam and Cologne, they arrived at Frankfurt, where they were refused admittance, because they had no passports. It so happened, however, that Peter Boehler's father was resident in the city. They sent a messenger to him, and he came immediately, procured an entrance for them, and entertained them in the most friendly manner.

On Tuesday, July 4th, they arrived at Marienborn, the chief centre of the Brethren after Herrnhut.[5] Wesley reports that at this time it consisted of about ninety persons, gathered out of many nations. They were then living in a large house hired by

[1] Cf. Curnock, op. cit. Vol. i. pp. 152ff.; 169ff., 372ff.
[2] Cf. Cranz, op. cit. p. 228.
[3] See supra, p. 88; Cf. Curnoch, op. cit. Vol. ii. pp. 4n. 62
[4] Cf. Curnock. op. cit. Vol. ii. p. 5.
[5] See *supra*, pp. 91ff., 93ff.

the count, but were building another one about three English miles off, on the top of a fruitful hill. This was Herrnhaag to which reference has already been made.[1] Wesley comments, 'Oh, how pleasant a thing it is for brethren to dwell together in unity!'[2]

At Marienborn Wesley spent a fortnight, and lodged with one of the Brethren at Eckershausen, an English mile from Marienborn, where he usually spent the day, chiefly with those who could speak Latin or English, as he himself, for lack of practice, was unable to speak German readily. Here, he reports, he continually met with what he sought, namely, living proofs of the power of faith: persons saved from inward and outward sin by 'the love of God shed abroad in their hearts,' and from all doubt and fear by the abiding witness of 'the Holy Ghost given unto them.'[3] He also heard Zinzendorf preach in the old castle at Ronneberg (about three English miles from Marienborn).

A few days later he attended one of the conferences for strangers and heard the count speak at large upon the subject which had been proposed for discussion, namely, Can a man be justified and not know it? He compared what the count said with what Peter Boehler had said to him on the same subject. At Ingham's request he stayed a little longer at Marienborn than he had intended. On Wednesday, the 19th of July, he resumed his journey with a Mr. Hauptmann, a native of Dresden, and another companion.

After travelling for several days they called at Jena, the *Alma Mater* of Peter Boehler and Spangenberg. Wesley speaks highly of the brotherly kindness with which they were here received. On the second day after leaving Jena they came to Halle, which Wesley specially desired to see. This was the place where Zinzendorf had received his early education. Reference has already been made to the institutions which had there been established by professor Francke.[4] As the travellers had some difficulty in obtaining admittance to the town, Wesley sent a note to pro-

---

[1] See *supra*, p. 93; See also *infra*, pp. 135ff.
[2] Cf. Curnock, op. cit. Vol. ii. pp. 10f.
[3] Ibid. Vol. ii. p. 13.
[4] See *supra*, pp. 65f.

fessor Francke. Though he was not in town, the travellers were eventually admitted to the Orphan House, 'that amazing proof that all things are still possible to him that believeth.' Curnock points out that this is the origin of the Orphan Houses of both Wesley and Whitefield.[1] Wesley refers to various other institutions which had been established there — printing-office, bookroom, and an apothecary's shop.

Passing through Leipzig, Meissen, Dresden and Neustadt, on Tuesday, August 1st, they came to Herrnhut, about thirty English miles from Dresden. Wesley reports that at that time it contained about a hundred houses. It had one long street, through which passed the road from Zittau to Lobau. Fronting the middle of the street was the Orphan House; in the lower part of which was the apothecary's shop, in the upper part the chapel, capable of containing six or seven hundred people. He describes Zinzendorf's house as a 'small plain building like the rest; having a large garden behind it, well laid out, not for show, but for the use of the community.'[2]

The visitors had a convenient lodging assigned them in the house appointed for strangers. Wesley rejoiced to find here Mr. Hermsdorf, with whom he had often conversed in Georgia; and remarks that his friend did all in his power to make their stay useful and agreeable.

I shall not attempt to give in any detail Wesley's report of life as he found it at Herrnhut. For a fuller account the inquiring reader may be referred to the Standard Edition of Wesley's *Journal*, which contains a long and very interesting narrative, with numerous illustrations.[3] The editor supplements Wesley's report with useful notes giving information concerning many of the leading personalities, already mentioned in our account of the Brethren's Church: e.g. Martin Dober, Polycarp Müller, Christian David, J. A. Rothe, and many others.

The day after his arrival Wesley attended a love-feast of the married men. During the days which followed he embraced every opportunity of sharing in the varied life of the community, being present at the conference for strangers, Bible confer-

---

[1] Cf. op. cit. Vol. ii. p. 17 (note).
[2] Cf. Curnock, op. cit. Vol. ii. p. 19.
[3] Ibid. Vol. ii. pp. 20—63; See also *supra*, pp. 7off., 76ff.

ences, and other meetings for fellowship. He had much conversation with the most experienced of the Brethren concerning
the work which God had wrought in their souls. Two days
after Wesley reached the place, Christian David arrived. Wesley heard him preach four times, and listened to him with
eager attention.[1] Of the first sermon he immediately afterwards
wrote down the substance. It is remarked that each time Christian David preached he chose just the subject which Wesley
could have wished.

Wesley also gives long accounts of conversations which he
had with several of the more experienced and prominent elders
of the Church, e.g. Michael Linner, David Nitschmann, Augustin Wenzel, Hans Neisser, and David Schneider; whilst his
report of the constitution, regulations, and general discipline
of the Brethren occupies many pages.[2]

On the Sunday the visitors attended service in the church at
Bertholdsdorf, of which Wesley gives a detailed account. He
relates also that after the evening service at Herrnhut, all the
unmarried men (as was their custom) walked round the town,
singing praise, with instruments of music; and then, on a small
hill, a short distance away, joined in prayer. Several evenings
during this week Wesley attended one or other of the private
bands, a type of meeting of a very similar character to the
classes and bands which later became one of the most characteristic features of Methodism.

Wesley spent nearly a fortnight among the Brethren at
Herrnhut. He found their fellowship congenial and a spiritual
tonic. 'I would gladly have spent my life here,' he says, 'but
my Master calling me to labour in another part of His vine-
yard, on Monday, 14th (August), I was constrained to take my
leave of this happy place, Martin Döber, and a few others of
the Brethren, walking with us about an hour. Oh, when shall
this Christianity cover the earth, as the "waters cover the sea"?'

Wesley reached London on Saturday, September 16th, 1738,
a month after he left Herrnhut. He had been absent from England three months. About a month after his return he wrote

[1] Ibid. Vol. ii. pp. 28ff.
[2] Ibid. Vol. ii. pp. 49ff.
[3] Cf. Telford, op. cit. p. 110.

a letter to Zinzendorf at Marienborn, thanking him and the countess for their kindness, and which he closed by saying, 'The love and the zeal of our Brethren in Holland and Germany, particularly at Herrnhuth, have stirred up many among us, who will not be comforted till they also partake of the great and precious promises. I hope to see them at least once more, were it only to speak freely of a few things which I did not approve, perhaps because I did not understand them.'[1]

An indication of the nature of some of the things which Wesley did not approve is given in an unfinished letter to the Moravians at Marienborn and Herrnhut which Wesley wrote (but for some reason did not send), a few days after his return. It reads: 'My Dear Brethren,—I cannot but rejoice in your steadfast faith, in your love to our blessed Redeemer, your deadness to the world, your meekness, temperance, chastity, and love of one another. I greatly approve of your conferences and bands; of your methods of instructing children; and, in general, of your great care of the souls committed to your charge.

'But of some other things I stand in doubt, which I will mention in love and meekness . . .

'Is not the count all in all among you?

'Do you not magnify your own Church too much?

'Do you not use guile and dissimulation in many cases?

'Are you not of a close, dark, reserved temper and behaviour?'[2]

It is well known that, as the years passed, Wesley's objections to various features of Moravianism found free and full expression. As already remarked, it is not altogether surprising that two such great religious leaders as Wesley and Zinzendorf could not run in harness together. A little later we shall notice some of the points of divergence between the two great movements of which they were the leaders.

---

[1] Cf. Tyerman, op. cit. Vol. i. p. 206.
[2] Ibid. Vol. i. p. 207; See also Wesley's *Works*, Vol. viii. pp. 365.

CHAPTER FIFTEEN

From the Synod of Gotha in 1740 to Zinzendorf's Return from America in 1743

IN 1740 a Synod was held at Gotha at which many important matters relating to the future work of the Church were considered. At this Synod, Zinzendorf, having mentioned the reproaches which were cast upon him, and the unfavourable impression which existed in the minds of some divines and statesmen on account of his uniting in his own person the titles of count and Moravian bishop, begged to be discharged from his episcopal functions; and that someone might take his place. The Brethren, however, represented to him that so long as the Church sought to please Jesus it would not fail to incur the hatred of the world. As he continued to press the matter, though they would not accept his resignation, they elected another bishop, namely, the Rev. Polycarp Müller, a Lutheran divine, who had formerly filled a professorial chair at the University of Leipzig.[1]

At the same Synod the Brethren spent much time in considering what ought to be the special mode of their operation as a Church. They reached the conclusion that they ought to be a 'Free Congregation of Jesus,' and to work in free union with other Churches. They were to be like salt in the earth and to care for the scattered people of God everywhere. They were to make no attempt to proselytise from other branches of the Church; but to adopt rather the method called 'Diaspora,' whereby Christian people should be formed into 'Societies,' without attaching them to the Brethren's Church.

In 1741 another important question came up for discussion. Leonard Dober, who for some years had been the chief elder of the Church, laid down his office; and the question arose as to

[1] Cf. Bost, op. cit. p. 355; Cranz, op. cit. p. 248.

who should succeed him as chief elder. The matter was considered at a conference in London. After careful consideration, and after studying their book of texts, it was decided that Christ alone should be regarded as their chief elder. This meant that henceforth the rule of one man was abolished; there was to be no earthly chief elder. Instead of this, a Conference of Twelve was elected, and the Church was freed from the danger of a Papacy. True, the Headship of Christ had been their doctrine from the beginning. It now became a realized fact, and means were taken to make it practically operative in the life of the Church. The decision was taken on September 16th, 1741; and was made known to the Congregations on the 13th November. This has ever since been kept as a Memorial Day in the Church of the Brethren.[1]

During this same year Zinzendorf paid a visit to Geneva, arriving there early in March. He was accompanied by the countess and his family, together with forty or fifty Brethren, who were lodged in several houses near his residence. Together they formed a little Church, regularly organized in their usual fashion. The count's aim on this visit was to become better acquainted with the Church of Calvin, the mother of many Presbyterian Churches, and to enter into friendly conversation with this Church. At the same time he was willing to serve his friends in Switzerland who desired to be visited by the Brethren. He had many conversations with professors and ministers, and put into their hands a narrative of the origin, regulations and discipline of the Brethren's Church. He likewise ordered some important documents to be deposited in the library, as he had sometimes done elsewhere. All this was well received, as appears from a eulogy and good wishes which were presented by a deputation from the university and clergy.

Some dissatisfaction, however, was felt with a writing issued to defend the orthodoxy of the Brethren on the subject of the Trinity; and also with a regulation which prohibited all strangers from attending his meetings. On this account, and to avoid any disturbance, the count and his whole household left the city in the month of May and returned to Wetteravia.[2]

[1] Cf. Hutton, op. cit. pp. 173ff.; Cranz, op. cit. pp. 254f.
[2] Cf. Cranz, op. cit. pp. 252f.; Bost, op. cit. pp. 362ff.

Zinzendorf was contemplating making another visit to America, in view of which another synodal conference was held at Marienborn in June and July. At this Synod he announced, as he had already done at Gotha, his desire to lay down his office as bishop. He thought it might be prejudicial to his intended labour in Pennsylvania, where he wished to appear simply as a Lutheran divine. Further, he felt called to give himself more and more to the work of an evangelist; in a way he could not do while bound by the ties of office to one section of the Church. Thereupon John Nitschmann, inspector of the seminary, was elected bishop and consecrated at Herrnhaag.[1]

Having arranged these things, on August 5th Zinzendorf, with his eldest daughter Henrietta Benigna Justina, set out on his second visit to America. He arrived in New York on the 2nd December, 1741. He first went to Philadelphia, and then travelled through the chief districts of the province of Pennsylvania, where the Germans lived, in order to become acquainted with the state of religion in the country. This he found confused and deplorable in the last degree. There were Episcopalians, Schwenkfelders, Independents, Quakers, Baptists, Mennonites or Anabaptists, Presbyterians, Seventh-Day men, and various other sects. The intention of the count was to serve the German Lutherans, who had no teachers or ordained ministers. Most of the ministers who had come out to Pennsylvania had died. The children grew up in the woods without instruction, and most of them without baptism. Some of the Germans had joined the other sects.[2]

At an earlier date, in 1736, these people had been visited by Spangenberg, after he had regulated the colony in Georgia, and also by bishop David Nitschmann. But as early as 1740 the last Brethren from Georgia had retreated thither. The Methodist Rev. George Whitefield had bought a piece of land in Pennsylvania, which he called Nazareth, intending to build there a school for the negroes. He desired the Brethren to view the land, and to take upon them the care of the building: the offer

[1] Ibid. pp. 253f.; Bost, op. cit. p. 366.
[2] Cf. Cranz, op. cit. pp. 256ff.; Bost, op. cit. p. 366.

H

was accepted. This meant that the Brethren could live together, instead of being scattered among the various sects.

Another piece of land was offered them in 1740, just when bishop David Nitschmann arrived with his company. They decided to accept it and to build a settlement there. A beginning was made in March 1741. When Zinzendorf arrived there at the end of the year, a small farmhouse and a stable were finished. The congregation-house was not yet habitable. On this account Christmas was celebrated in the stable. When the question arose as to what they should call the place, they called to mind the birth of Jesus in another stable, and decided to call it Bethlehem. Shortly after Whitefield found it necessary to sell his land with the house half finished.[1] The Brethren accepted the offer to purchase and finished the house in 1743. Both Bethlehem and Nazareth became strong Moravian settlements.[2]

The Lutherans at Philadelphia had fitted up a barn for their public worship. In this the Reformed Church also had its services every fourth Sunday in the month. The Lutherans desired to hear Zinzendorf, and he preached on several Sundays. Afterwards they gave him a call to be their minister. This he accepted under the name of Mons. de Thuernstein, a divine of Tubingen, which was one of the titles of the counts of Zinzendorf. He also supplied other Lutheran congregations, and for a time he became the inspector of the Lutheran community in Pennsylvania. He likewise preached in the pulpits of the Reformed Church.[3]

The count and the Brethren took the lead in trying to establish more agreement among the various German sects in Pennsylvania, though not with the idea of getting them to join the Moravian Church. A circular letter was sent out on December 15th, 1741, desiring them to send deputies to a General Meeting at Germantown, in order to see how near they could come together on fundamental points, and to establish what was

---

[1] Cf. Tyerman, *The Life of George Whitefield*, Vol. i. p. 382.

[2] Cf. Cranz, op. cit. pp. 258f.; Hutton, op. cit. p. 216; For later developments at these places, see Hamilton, J. T. *A History of the Church Known as the Moravian Church or Unitas Fratrum Etc. during the 18th. and 19th. Centuries* (1900), pp. 138ff. and passim.

[3] Cf. Cranz, op. cit. p. 260.

called a 'Congregation of God in the Spirit.' Several such conferences were held. After a promising beginning, however, they
came to nothing.[1]

In addition to the settlements at Bethlehem and Nazareth,
others were established at Lititz and Salem. Schools were built
for poor children, each being placed under the care of a married
couple. In seven of the thirteen original States Societies were
founded which afterwards became Congregations (in the Moravian sense of the word).

Hutton is probably right in his view that it was a mistake
on the part of Zinzendorf and his associates to carry over the
method of founding settlements from Europe to the New
World.[2] The situation in America was completely different
from that in Germany. In Germany there was a National
Church, to which everyone was supposed to belong. In America
no such Church existed. The Brethren would have been well
advised to abandon the settlement system, and to have founded
Congregations or Churches, rather than mere Societies. When
members at the preaching-places applied for admission they
took them into the settlements; they should rather have gone
boldly forward and allowed the Church to spread.

The most fruitful work of the Brethren was that carried
on among the Indians. The leader of this work for some years
had been Christian Henry Rauch. Zinzendorf made three jour-
neys among them.[3] The last of these was begun on 24th September, 1742, and passed through untrodden paths, over steep and
dangerous mountains, across rivers, and through woods which
abounded with wild beasts and serpents. A plot was made to
murder him, but it was fortunately discovered in time by his
interpreter, Conrad Weisser.

Having done all he could to unite the Christian forces in the
colony, and having settled a congregation of the Brethren at
Bethlehem, and made preparation for a colony at Nazareth;
and likewise visited the mission stations among the heathen,
the count gave a farewell discourse at Philadelphia to his

[1] Cf. Cranz, op. cit. pp. 263ff.; Hutton, op. cit. pp. 216f.
[2] Cf. Hutton, op. cit. p. 218.
[3] Cf. Cranz, op. cit. pp. 266, 267, 269.

fellow-labourers on the 9th of January, 1743, and set out by way of New York on his return to Europe.[1]

The dangerous character of the work which was undertaken by the Brethren in N. America from this time onwards may be illustrated by the fact that on one occasion a band of missionaries was attacked by Indians while they were sitting at supper in a little house at Gnadenhütten. Bishop David Nitschmann was shot dead on the spot. Three of his companions escaped; one was scalped alive, and the rest roasted to death. Yet the Brethren did not hesitate to continue their work. One of the noblest figures of the period was David Zeisberger, a member of an old Moravian family, who had come with his father to Herrnhut in May, 1724. For sixty years he lived among the Indians, and became almost an Indian, and a member of an Indian family. He began his work among what were known as the Six Nations. He so completely won the confidence of these suspicious savages that he was allowed to move among them at will. The 'Six Nations' passed laws to ensure that he might continue his work without interruption. The result was that their mode of life was remodelled, and they learned to govern their own little townships like an English Local Board.

Unfortunately, when his work had thus been crowned with success, war broke out between England and her colonies. Each party wished the Indians to take up arms on its side. Zeisberger had taught them to lay aside their arms, and to live peaceably together. Each side accused him of being in league with its enemies. At last American troops appeared at Gnadenhütten. The log huts were turned into shambles: and ninety corpses lay on the ground. When Zeisberger died he saw nothing but ruin about him. Of his settlements only two—New Salem and Fairfield—remained. He breathed his last with a company of Indians around him.[2]

Zinzendorf arrived in England on 17th February, 1743, with a company of twenty persons. Having attended to affairs in London, he went on into Yorkshire, and visited parts about Leeds and Halifax, where, since 1739, a great work had been

[1] Cf. Cranz, op. cit. pp. 270f.
[2] Cf. Hutton, op. cit. pp. 221ff.; Cranz, op. cit. pp. 330, 383, 423, 591.

carried on by the Rev. Benjamin Ingham, and several other Brethren.[1] On his return to London, he visited Dr. Potter, the Archbishop of Canterbury, who still maintained his favourable attitude to the Brethren. He also deposited in the Library at Lambeth Palace the original writings concerning the correspondence with the Creek Church. Among others whom he visited at this time was George Whitefield.[2]

At the beginning of April Zinzendorf arrived in Holland. After conference with the bishops and elders whom he met at Amsterdam, where he also found his eldest son, Christian Renatus, he went on to Wetteravia. and arrived at Herrnhaag at the end of the month.[3]

[1] Cf. Cranz, op. cit. p. 273.
[2] Ibid. p. 274.
[3] Ibid. p. 275.

CHAPTER SIXTEEN

The Brethren in London

ANY attempt to give even the briefest account of the progress of the work done by the Church of the United Brethren in England will compel us to take note of the many relationships that were established between the Moravian Brethren and the Methodists in London and elsewhere. Some of the early contacts have already been indicated; and we have seen how deeply Wesley appreciated the guidance and inspiration which he received, in particular, from Peter Boehler and Gottlieb Spangenberg; whilst his visit to the headquarters of the Church of the Brethren in Germany gave him many ideas as to organization, discipline and fellowship which soon found expression in the formation and building up of the United Methodist Societies.

One of the earliest and most important links between the two movements is to be found in the person of James Hutton, of Westminster. At Oxford Hutton had met the Wesley brothers, and had invited them to visit him. His father was an ordained minister of the Church of England, but had resigned his church preferments, as he was unable to take the necessary oaths at the accession of King George I. He had begun a boarding-school in a house next door to that of Wesley's brother Samuel. He was a devout old man, and here Wesley preached a sermon on 'One thing is Needful,' which was the means of converting both James and his sister.[1] James Hutton became one of the principal Moravians in England.

We have already noticed the presence of John Wesley at the first meeting of a small society which met in Hutton's house, in little Wild Street, near Temple Bar, on May 1st, 1738. It had been formed on the advice of Peter Boehler. It should be noticed that meetings of this character within the Anglican Church were well known at this time.[2] They were therefore

[1] Cf. Tyerman, *The Life and Times of John Wesley*, Vol. i. p. 108.
[2] Cf. Telford, op. cit. pp. 145ff.; Curnock, op. cit. Vol. i. p. 458n.

not peculiar to the Methodists or to the Moravians. though
both these made much use of them. In his Oxford days Wesley
had said to a 'serious man': 'Sir, you are to serve God and go
to heaven. Remember you cannot serve Him alone: you must
therefore find companions or make them: the Bible knows
nothing of solitary religion.'[1] Count Zinzendorf expressed himself to the same effect. After preaching one day to a great
crowd in Berlin, he had a conversation with a young
lieutenant. He said to him, 'Let me ask you one question. Are
you alone in your religious troubles, or do you share them with
others?' The lieutenant replied that he and some companions
were accustomed to pray together. 'That is right,' exclaimed
Zinzendorf, 'I acknowledge no Christianity without fellowship.'[2] We have seen that meetings for fellowship in classes
and bands had long been a prominent characteristic of the
Church of the United Brethren.

When the house of James Hutton became too small for the
meetings of the society, they removed to the chapel at 32
Fetter Lane.[3] Of this society Wesley was one of the original
members. After Peter Boehler had left England, the society was
under the care of the two Wesleys. It made steady progress,
fed continually by Wesley's preaching. Soon, however, the
situation there was disturbed by the arrival, on 18th October,
1739, of Philip Henry Molther, a Moravian minister, who was
on his way to Pennsylvania. He was invited to preach, and
soon became exceedingly popular. Within a fortnight after his
arrival, Wesley came from Bristol, 'and the first person he met
was one whom he had left strong in faith, and zealous of good
works; but who now told him, that Molther had fully convinced her she had never had any faith at all, and had advised
her, till she received faith, to be still, ceasing from outward
works.' This was on November 1st, 1739.[4]

It should be observed that the society at Fetter Lane was
not a Moravian society. It had no connection with them till

[1] Ibid. p. 147.
[2] Cf. Hutton, op. cit. p. 172.
[3] Or "to a room in Fetter Lane." Curnock says that "The chapel was not
leased by Hutton until after the disruption." Cf. Curnock, op. cit. Vol. i. p.
458n.
[4] Cf. Tyerman, op. cit. Vol. i. p. 297.

Molther's arrival, except in the personal friendship and sympathy of its leading members. The Wesleys were never Moravians, nor members of a Moravian society, as has sometimes been supposed. Molther's visit marked the beginning of the conversion of the Fetter Lane society into a Moravian society.[1]

Disagreement between the Methodists and the Moravians appears first to have sprung up on the question of the right use of the means of grace. Curnock remarks that a few days after Molther's arrival in London, he was introduced to the Fetter Lane society by Hutton, who, on his return from visiting Zinzendorf (October 24th), 'was anxious to bring the society under Moravian teaching. Molther was an instrument ready to hand. He taught a kind of 'Quietism' called 'stillness,' and succeeded in persuading many of the members that the faith which they professed to have in Christ was not the true faith, and that they must remain 'still,' without using the 'so-called' means of grace, until they received faith.'[2]

Entries in Wesley's *Journal* for November 1st, 1739, set the root of the trouble clearly before us. He says, 'In the evening Mr. Bray also was highly commending the being 'still' before the Lord. He likewise spoke largely of the great danger that attended the doing of outward works, and of the folly of people that keep running about to Church and to Sacrament, 'as I,' said he, 'did till very lately.' On Sunday 4th, his entry runs:— 'Our society met at seven in the morning, and continued silent till eight. One (Spangenberg) then spoke of looking unto Jesus, and exhorted us all to lie still in His hand. In the evening I met the women of our society at Fetter Lane, where some of our brethren strongly intimated that none of them had any true faith, and then asserted, in plain terms: (1) that, till they had true faith, they ought to be 'still'; that is (as they explained themselves), to abstain from the means of grace, as they are called—the Lord's Supper in particular;

---

[1] Cf. Telford, op. cit. pp. 148f.; Curnock, op. cit. Vol. i., p. 458(note); Benham, D., *Memoirs of James Hutton* (1856), pp. 53ff.; Hutton, op. cit. pp. 184, 186.
[2] Cf. Curnock, op. cit. Vol. ii. p. 312 (note).

(2) that the ordinances are not means of grace, there being no other means than Christ.'[1]

Anxious to understand the situation thoroughly, on November 7th, Wesley had a long conference with Spangenberg. He agreed with all that the latter said about the power of faith, but he could not agree 'either that none has any faith so long as he is liable to any doubt or fear; or, that till we have it, we ought to abstain from the Lord's Supper or the other ordinances of God.'[2]

During the days which followed Wesley pondered deeply over the teaching of Molther and his associates, and summed up his own belief in these words: '(1) that there are means of grace—that is, outward ordinances—whereby the inward grace of God is ordinarily conveyed to man, whereby the faith that brings salvation is conveyed to them who before had it not; (2) that one of these means is the Lord's Supper; and (3) that he who has not this faith ought to wait for it in the use both of this and of the other means which God hath ordained.'[3]

Leaving the society at London in this divided and unsatisfactory state, Wesley went on his travels, visiting, among other places, Wycombe, Oxford, Tiverton, Bristol and Exeter. Everywhere he sought to show the nature of saving grace, and of the faith by which we are saved; admitting that a man might use the means of grace, and do much good, and yet have no religion at all.

On his return to London he had a long and particular conversation with Molther, and by much questioning he endeavoured to make sure of the exact meaning of his teaching. In his *Journal*, under date December 31st, 1739, he summarises their differences under five heads. These centre round the belief in degrees of faith, the nature of justifying faith, the full assurance of faith, and the use of the means of grace to attain faith. Neither was convinced by the arguments of the other. On the following day Wesley endeavoured to explain to the brethren the true, Christian, scriptural stillness, by unfold-

[1] Ibid. Vol. ii. pp. 313f.
[2] Ibid. Vol. ii. p. 314.
[3] Ibid. Vol. ii. p. 315.

ing the meaning of the words, 'Be still, and know that I am God.' The day but one after he set out upon his travels.[1]

The disputings which have been indicated were not confined to the Fetter Lane society. They were gradually spread far and wide. During the tour which Wesley undertook following the conversation with Molther he found at Reading the same kind of disputation. He says, 'I now found some from London had been here, grievously troubling these souls also; labouring to persuade them (1) that they had no faith at all, because they sometimes felt doubt and fear; and (2) that they ought to be still; not to go to church, not to communicate, not to search the Scriptures; 'because,' they say, 'you cannot do any of these things without trusting in them.'[2]

On various occasions after this Wesley visited Fetter Lane and discussed the subject in dispute with Molther and others;[3] but it was impossible to make any progress in the way of harmonising the contradictory teachings.

Before considering the action which Wesley was presently led to take, it will be advisable to take note of the fact that other things were involved besides the difference in doctrinal teaching. There was the question of leadership. We have seen that the society at Fetter Lane was originally a society within the Church of England; and that for some time it was under the pastoral care of the two Wesleys. Hutton, however, a prominent member, was a Moravian. Curnock says that soon after the arrival of Molther Hutton was anxious to bring the society under Moravian teaching.[4] As supporting this view, we may point to a letter written by Hutton to Zinzendorf, dated March 14th, 1740. In this letter there are certain expressions which seem clearly to show that there was jealousy of Wesley's leadership. He speaks of John Wesley as being 'resolved to do all things himself . . .'; 'envy,' he says, 'is not extinct in him . . . . ' 'I desired him simply to keep to his office in the body of Christ, i.e. to awaken souls in preaching, but not to pretend to lead them to Christ. But he will have the

[1] Ibid. Vol. ii. pp. 328ff., 331.
[2] Cf. Curnock, op. cit. Vol. ii. p. 337.
[3] Ibid. Vol. ii. pp. 343f., 352.
[4] Cf. supra, p. 120.

glory of doing all things . . . . '[1] It is quite evident from this
that there were those who were prepared to challenge the
leadership of Wesley in favour of that of Molther and his
associates.

In addition to these differences with regard to teaching and
leadership, there was a difference in the mode of giving expression to Gospel truth. The Brethren had come to use language
which may not unfairly be described as mawkish senti-
mentality. Hutton speaks of the years 1743-50 as the 'Sifting
Time.' In those days, he says, there was a spiritual fever in
the air, and the Brethren caught the disease. They had mixed
so much with strange and foolish people in Wetteravia that
they became strange and foolish themselves. They revelled in
sentimental language. Like those around them, they called
themselves 'little fools', 'Virgins', that were only to enjoy
themselves 'in the wounds of Jesus.' They also wrote hymns
giving gruesome descriptions of the crucified Saviour.

Another expression of the unhealthy spiritual condition of
the time was the frivolous use made of the Lot to decide such
things as, whether they should go to a meeting or build a
house; or whether certain opinions were right or wrong.[2]

In illustration of the language used by the Brethren at this
time we may cite two expressions from a letter written by
Molther to Wesley on January 25th, 1740. He says: 'I love you
with a real love in the wounds of the Redeemer;' and near the
end of the letter he expresses the wish 'that our Saviour, for
His own sake, may . . . . fill up your heart with a solid knowledge of His bloody atonement.' In another letter Zinzendorf
speaks of Doddridge as 'the very reverend man, much beloved
in the bowels of the blessed Redeemer.'[3]

There is no lack of intense spiritual feeling in the hymns
and other writings of the Wesleys; but we may be thankful that
they were preserved from expressions of this kind.

Incidents occurred which continually aggravated the situation. Charles Wesley saw that separation was unavoidable. On

---

[1] Cf. Tyerman, op. cit. Vol. i. p. 299; Benham, D., *Memoirs of James
Hutton*, pp. 46f.

[2] Hutton, op. cit. pp. 175f.; See also Cranz, op. cit. pp. 370ff.

[3] Cf. Tyerman, op. cit. Vol. i. pp. 298f., 300.

Easter Day, 1740, when preaching at the Foundery, he appealed to the society, and asked, 'Who hath bewitched you, that you should let go your Saviour, and deny you ever knew Him?' Expressions of sorrow followed; but on going to meet the bands in the evening the door was shut against him, and proceeding to Mr. Bray's, one of the members, he was threatened with expulsion from the Moravian society. In a society meeting at the Foundery J. Bray declared that it was 'impossible for anyone to be a true Christian out of the Moravian Church.'[1]

Wesley preached a series of sermons dealing with all the main points in dispute. Benjamin Ingham and Howell Harris 'honestly withstood the deluded Brethren.' The result was only increased commotion. After a short debate Wesley was prohibited from preaching in Fetter Lane. As Tyerman remarks, 'the man who had founded the Fetter Lane society was now, by Moravian votes, commanded to go about his business, and to leave the pulpit to his German superiors.'[2]

Matters had now reached a crisis. Wesley was compelled to take decisive action. If, as Tyerman says, the Fetter Lane society did not exclude Wesley from their membership, they, on the 16th of July, 1740, expelled him from their pulpit. Four days afterwards, he went with Mr. Seward to their love-feast, and, at its conclusion, read a paper stating the errors into which they had fallen, and concluding thus:— 'I believe these assertions to be flatly contrary to the word of God. I have warned you hereof again and again, and besought you to turn back to the 'law and the testimony.' I have borne with you long, hoping you would turn. But, as I find you more and more confirmed in the error of your ways, nothing now remains, but that I should give you up to God. You that are of the same judgement, follow me.'

Wesley then silently withdrew, followed by eighteen or nineteen members of the society. The day after, the seceding society, to the number of about twenty-five men and fifty women, met for the first time at the Foundery, instead of at

[1] Ibid. Vol. i. pp. 302f.
[2] Ibid, Vol. i. pp. 307f.

Fetter Lane. Thus the Methodist Society was founded on July 23rd, 1740.[1]

As the years passed by other things happened to exacerbate the feelings of bitterness that were engendered in the way that has been indicated. Into these we shall not enter here. It is important, however, to note that Wesley saw quite clearly at this time that the whole Moravian Church should not be held responsible for these lamentable and tragic divisions. On September 29th, 1740, Wesley, having stated what the errors were, and affirming that a man may use the ordinances of God, the Lord's Supper in particular, before he has a perfect faith, says, 'I further assert, that I learned this, not only from the English, but also from the Moravian Church; and I hereby openly and earnestly call upon that Church, and upon count Zinzendorf in particular, to correct me, and explain themselves, if I have misunderstood or misrepresented them.' Tyerman says with truth that Wesley puts the blame on the right shoulders. 'It was not the Moravian *Church*, but a few of its foolish ministers and members, at Fetter Lane, that circulated these heresies.'[2]

Tyerman's judgement is in accord with the evidence presented in the preceding chapters. The doctrine of 'stillness' finds no place in the earlier teaching of the United Brethren. We have seen how the Brethren found the Sacrament of the Lord's Supper so helpful that they asked for a more frequent celebration.[3] Though they were a simple and spiritual-minded community, and cultivated a homely type of fellowship, there was no objection to ordinances on the ground of 'stillness.'

We cannot here explain fully the source or sources of these erronous ideas, which Wesley found so repugnant and harmful. One probable source is contact with the Quakers. In a

[1] Cf. Tyerman, op. cit. Vol. i., pp. 309f. The Foundery was an old building which had been formerly used for the recasting of cannon taken by Marlborough from the French. It had been wrecked in 1716 by an explosion. It was bought by Wesley as a preaching-place, and adapted for Methodist purposes. It had been occupied by Wesley since November 11th., 1739. It served as the headquarters of Methodism until the City Road Chapel was built in 1778. See Curnock op. cit. Vol. ii. p. 316 (note); Telford, op. cit. p. 130.

[2] Op. cit. Vol. i. p. 309; Telford, op. cit. p. 138.

[3] Cf. *supra*, p. 76.

letter which Charles Wesley wrote to Whitefield in America, on September 1st, 1740, he refers to the trouble-makers at Fetter Lane, and says, 'The Quakers, they say, are exactly right; and, indeed, the principles of the one naturally lead to the other. For instance, take our friend Morgan. One week he and his wife were at J. Bray's, under the teaching of the *still* brethren. Soon after, he turned Quaker, and is now a celebrated preacher among them.'[1]

It should be remembered, however, that Quietism had had a long history before the days of George Fox. A useful and convenient summary of the teachings of both Christian and non-Christian Quietists is given by Blunt.[2] Another possible source is medieval mysticism, which may have been studied by more of the Moravian ministers than is known to us, Wesley relates how he and Spangenberg discussed mystical divinity, and states that the latter acknowledged himself a 'mystic.'

The separation of the Methodists from the Fetter Lane society led the pro-Moravian party to reorganize themselves as a 'Society of the Moravian Brethren.' After some months stewards were appointed, and, in October, 1742, Spangenberg, acting for Zinzendorf, constituted the Society of seventy-two persons a Church or Congregation of the Unity of the Brethren. William Holland was appointed elder, and James Hutton warden, and the usual rules and regulations were introduced.[3]

---

[1] Cf. Tyerman, op. cit. Vol. i. p. 311.
[2] Cf. *Sects, Heresies and Schools of Thought* (1874), pp. 471ff.
[3] Cf. Curnock, op. cit. Vol. ii. p. 370 (footnote); Hutton, op. cit. p. 187.

CHAPTER SEVENTEEN

The Brethren in Yorkshire and Elsewhere

DURING the time that the unhappy events which have been indicated were in progress the evangelistic work both of the Methodists and the Moravians continued to flourish. The two movements touched at many points, and sometimes there were clashes. A connected account of these belongs rather to the story of Methodism, and of the whole evangelical revival, than to our more limited subject. I shall here therefore endeavour to give only a brief account of the establishment of Moravian centres in this country, and of the nature of the work done by them, referring to other matters only in immediate connection with this theme.

First, we shall notice a number of interesting personalities who did much to extend the work of the Brethren. Mention has already been made of Benjamin Ingham, one of the associates of Wesley from his Oxford days. He was ordained, and went with Wesley to Georgia, returning to England in February 1737. He was likewise one of Wesley's companions on his visit to the Moravian headquarters in Germany in 1738. His family belonged to Yorkshire, and on his return from Germany he became an evangelical clergyman at Ossett, not far from Leeds. From that place, on February 20th, 1740, he wrote an interesting letter to Wesley, dealing with the questions which were then in debate among the Methodists and the Moravians.[1] He was manifestly a man of stirling character, greatly appreciated by Wesley, even after he had become associated with the Moravians.

As Tyerman observes, despite the events which have been recorded, Wesley entertained no bitterness towards the Moravians. He acknowledged that they had a desire to serve God, and that their discipline, in most respects, was excellent. At the same time he was forthright in his criticism of what he regarded as their errors. He strongly opposed suggestions for a

[1] Cf. Tyerman, op. cit. Vol. i. p. 306.

re-union between Wesley's London Society and the Moravians, which were made at Fetter Lane in 1741. He feared that his brother Charles was being affected by Moravian *stillness*, and wrote to him, saying, 'The Philistines are upon thee, Samson, but the Lord is not departed from thee.'[1]

Only a month after the London meeting Wesley made a tour among the Moravians in the midland counties, where Ingham had laboured with great success. It is, however, of Ingham's work in Yorkshire that I shall now speak more particularly; for there the institutions of the Brethren took deepest root. A colony or settlement of the Brethren, on the pattern of Herrnhut, was formed there, and, with modifications, this still remains.

The zeal of Ingham carried him far beyond the confines of his parish. He realized that there were thousands of people about him who knew little or nothing of the Gospel. The district between Halifax and Leeds, now containing many small manufacturing towns, was then wild moorland, dotted over with cottages and tiny hamlets. In this area Ingham travelled incessantly, preaching wherever he had an opportunity, and founding small societies, much after the pattern of Grimshaw of Haworth. In the space of a few years he had founded fifty small societies for prayer and Bible-reading.

Finding that the proper care of so many societies was beyond his capacity, it occurred to him to ask the Brethren to come and help him. He gathered all the members of his societies together in a large hall and put this question to them: 'Will you have the Moravians to work among you?' They heartily agreed, and Ingham wrote at once to London. The Brethren responded to the call; and soon twenty-six Brethren and Sisters were on the way thither, travelling in detachments. They made their headquarters at Smith House, near Wyke. Other main centres were Mirfield, Pudsey, Great Horton (Bradford), and Holbeck (Leeds). The general supervision was exercised by Spangenberg at Smith House. In each of these five divisions there was a central meeting-house, with smaller meeting-houses depending upon it. Before the Brethren had

[1] Ibid. p. 337.

JAMES HUTTON

been eighteen months in Yorkshire forty-seven preaching-places had been established.[1]

Meetings were held in cottages and barns, as well as in the meeting-houses. In common with the Methodists everywhere, the people—usually poor—were calumniated and suffered persecution. Bearing, as they did, a foreign name (though actually, like 'Methodist,' it was a nick-name, and not of their own choosing), the workers were often said to be spies and conspirators, and dragged before the justices. Many of their expressions, too, were a cause of stumbling to other Christian people. They asserted that only Christ could save them, and by His merits bestow upon them eternal life. There is, admittedly, a deep sense in which this is true; but, as frequently asserted, it involved a great danger of Antinomianism. The extent of this danger, at that time, can be discerned by anyone who will read the 'Checks to Antinomianism' written by Wesley's friend John Fletcher of Madely in Shropshire.

As illustrating the way in which the Brethren were misunderstood and maligned Hutton relates how the well-known Methodist lay-preacher, John Nelson, one day met a drunken man staggering along the road, and reproved him for his conduct. But the drunken man replied that he belonged to the Brethren, and that he was exactly as Christ wished him to be. Nelson went away with the impression that this was the real spirit of the Brethren.[2]

Those who have read the earlier chapters of this work will know that this does not truly represent the teaching of the Brethren. No large body of Christians has ever exercised a firmer moral discipline over its members than the Church of the United Brethren. We have seen how repeatedly they urged Luther to adopt a stricter discipline among his followers. But the mode in which even the leaders stated the Gospel lent itself to abuse and misunderstanding. In a conversation between Zinzendorf and Wesley, in September 1741, for example, certain statements made by the former seem to confuse justification and sanctification, imputed and inherent or realized righteousness. A man, Zinzendorf said, 'is not more holy if

[1] Cf. Cranz, op. cit. pp. 322, 399, 420; Hutton, op. cit. p. 192ff.
[2] Op. cit. p. 195.

I

he loves more, or less holy, if he loves less.' Again, he said, 'We reject all self-denial. We trample upon it. We do as believers, whatsoever we will, and nothing more.'[1] We are aware that the high authority of St. Augustine may be quoted for the saying that if 'you love God, you may do what you like.' But everything depends on what you mean by 'loving God,' and what by 'doing as you like.' So with the terms used by Zinzendorf. But the bald, unguarded statements were dangerous to the mass of the people who were not used to the scrutiny of terms.

As the work in Yorkshire flourished so mightily, reinforcements were requested, and John Toeltschig was sent to assist. He was a Moravian who had seen mission work in Georgia, and had travelled back to Germany in the company of John Wesley and Benjamin Ingham.[2] He later went to Ireland and worked in Dublin. He appears to have been a strong character and did much to build up the work in Yorkshire.

Ingham was the proprietor of Gracehill in Yorkshire. It was decided to build here, in the neighbourhood of Pudsey, and about six miles west of Leeds, a colony or settlement on the same pattern as Herrnhut. The work was regularly organized there in 1755.[3]

The new colony was called Fulneck, in memory of the place occupied by the Brethren in Moravia.[4] The spot was at that time a wild uncultivated hill, covered with briars and brambles. But help came from various sources; money from friends in Germany, and timber from friends in Norway. It was intended to be a Christian centre for preachers in the neighbourhood; also for missionaries as they moved to and from their stations. Between 1746 and 1771 a whole range of buildings was erected, including a chapel, minister's house, Brethren and Sisters' houses, widows' house, a shop and an inn; also a boys' boarding school. Each of the various congregations in the neighbourhood was independent, but looked to Fulneck as the centre.

---

[1] Cf. Tyerman, op. cit. Vol. i. p. 340.
[2] See *supra*, p. 106; cf. Cranz, op. cit. p. 228.
[3] Cf. Spangenberg, op. cit. p. 391; Bost, op. cit. p. 402.
[4] Ibid. p. 391. See *supra*, p. 51.

As the same system of government was established at Fulneck as at Herrnhut, we need not here go into detail. I will only add the further remark that each person engaged in business received a fixed salary, the profits of the business being devoted to Christian purposes.[1]

Another valiant worker of this period was John Cennick. He was born about 1718 in Berkshire, and came from an old Bohemian family, which had probably fled to England at the time of the downfall of the Ancient Church.[2] He made the acquaintance of Whitefield and the Wesleys at Oxford. As the school-master elect at Kingswood he began to preach there in June 1739. He had gone from Bristol to hear a young man read a sermon under a sycamore tree in Kingswood, but the young man did not turn up and Cennick reluctantly took his place. Wesley was urged to forbid his preaching, but refused to do so. For a time Cennick was constantly employed in the neighbourhood of Bristol. During the Calvinistic controversy he left Wesley for Whitefield.[3]

Breaking away from Whitefield, Cennick set out on his own career as a preacher in Wiltshire. In July 1740, by invitation of a country gentleman, he preached to a great crowd in the little town of Castlecombe, and before long he formed for himself a preaching circuit. He had many adventures. With his friend Howell Harris, for example, he was attacked by a mob at Swindon, and drenched by water from a fire engine. Similar experiences awaited them elsewhere. But their courage and eloquence continued to attract great crowds of people.

In 1742 a house was turned into a chapel at Tytherton. Numerous other societies were formed in the district. After four and a half years Cennick found that the work was beyond his capacity to manage and proposed to the societies to ask for the assistance of the Brethren. The Brethren responded, and soon a number of them, including Spangenberg and Boehler, went down to Wiltshire, mapped out the district, and carried on the work. Mainly by the preaching of Cennick Con-

[1] Cf. Hutton, op. cit. pp. 197f.; Bost, op. cit. pp. 402f.; Cranz, op. cit., p. 420.

[2] Ibid. p. 199.

[3] Cf. Telford, op. cit. pp. 214f.; Tyerman, op. cit. Vol. i. pp. 275, 295; Tyerman, *Life of George Whitefield*, Vol. i. pp. 467, 484.

gregations were established at Bath, Bristol, Tytherton, Kingswood and Malmesbury.[1]

For a time Cennick was associated with Whitefield in his work in London, and whilst there, in 1745, he definitely joined the United Brethren.[2] In June, 1746, he went to Dublin, and commenced preaching in the old Baptist Hall, in Skinner's Alley.[3] There his work bore rich fruit. With such effect did he preach that those who wished to hear him had to come two or three hours before the time of service. The yard as well as the chapel was crowded, and the tops of the houses, the walls and windows were often black with the listening multitudes.

In this great work Cennick had the powerful assistance of Benjamin La Trobe, a young student in connection with the Baptists who, having finished his studies in the University of Glasgow, went to Dublin and there became the leader of a little group of pious people which had been formed into a society by an English soldier in 1745. It was at the request of this society that Cennick went to Dublin.[4] It increased greatly and was organized as a Congregation of the Brethren's Church by Peter Boehler in 1750.

From Dublin Cennick passed to North Ireland (1748), where he laboured for five years with great success. He had a kindly manner, a ready wit, and much eloquence, and made friends on every side, though he likewise had his share of persecution. Zinzendorf called him 'Paul revived.' When his preaching days were done he handed over to the care of other Brethren some fifty societies. He also saw the establishment of a colony called Gracehill—the Herrnhut of the North of Ireland. Whilst still a young man, worn out with holy toil, he died in London in 1755.[5]

During the time that this rapid progress was being made it became apparent that the Church of the United Brethren suffered various disabilities because as yet it had no legal

---

[1] Cf. Hutton, op. cit. pp. 201ff.; Tyerman, *Life of George Whitefield*, Vol. ii. pp. 40ff.

[2] Cf. Tyerman, op. cit. Vol. ii. pp. 148, 158, 174.

[3] Cf. Tyerman, op. cit. Vol. ii. p. 238; Cf. Cranz, op. cit. pp. 323f.

[4] Cf. Tyerman, *Life and Times of Wesley*, Vol. i. pp. 556.

[5] Cf. Hutton, op. cit. pp. 203ff.

standing in English law. It was resolved therefore to take the necessary steps to secure for the Brethren the protection of the law for the enjoyment of their modes of worship. In this matter General Oglethorpe rendered them great assistance. First a petition was presented to Parliament for an examination of the affairs of the Church; subsequently a Bill was introduced and passed by both Houses of Parliament, and received the Royal Assent on June 6th, 1749. It was thought there might have been some objection on the part of the bishops; but at a meeting at Lambeth they had agreed not to oppose it in the House of Lords. By this Act the Church of the Brethren was recognized as 'An Ancient Protestant and Episcopal Church.' Free and full exercise of their worship and constitution was guaranteed; simple affirmation in the name of Almighty God was allowed them instead of an oath; and under certain conditions they were exempted from military service.[1]

These legal proceedings did much good, since the falsity of many of the charges made against the Brethren was clearly demonstrated.

[1] Cf. Cranz, op. cit. pp. 349ff.; Bost, op. cit. p. 404; Hutton, op. cit. pp. 211ff.; Tyerman, *Life and Times of Wesley*, Vol. ii. pp. 97f.

CHAPTER EIGHTEEN

Difficulties at Herrnhaag, and in England: Death of Zinzendorf

ZINZENDORF lived in exile for ten years. During this period he paid two visits to America, spent a considerable time in England, particularly in London, and did much work on the Continent. Whilst on the Continent he made his home at Marienborn and Herrnhaag, whence he travelled to many distant places. We have seen that Herrnhaag was established in 1738, to be a place of asylum for persecuted people, particularly for those from Reformed countries, and to be a resting-place for missionaries passing to and from their stations.[1] The Congregation there increased rapidly, and in a few years it exceeded that at Herrnhut. In 1743 the first contract for the place was cancelled and a new one was made, and signed by the count of Issenberg Buedingen and his three sons. In this deed the Moravian Brethren's Church was acknowledged as an orthodox Protestant Congregation. For a time Zinzendorf lived at Marienborn and ministered the Gospel to the Congregations at Herrnhaag and Ronneberg.

In 1747 a Synod was held at Herrnhaag. Here Zinzendorf had built a house and a spacious chapel: he had left Marienborn to take up residence there at the beginning of the year. Several misunderstandings had now begun to appear between the regency of Buedingen and the directors of the colony at Herrnhaag; but as yet the colony was flourishing. At the Synod two new bishops were consecrated, one being Leonard Dober, the other John de Watteville, who married Zinzendorf's eldest daughter.[2]

The end of the count's exile was now very near. In 1747 an inquiry was instituted into his case, with the result that a royal decree was issued, which re-instated him in all his former

[1] Cf. *supra*, pp. 93, 107.
[2] Cf. Cranz, op. cit. pp. 276, 334, 336.

privileges. Before he availed himself, however, of this decree he procured another commission of inquiry into the affairs of the Church, which was still being calumniated. The result of the inquiry was favourable, and a royal charter was issued, dated September 20th, 1749, empowering the Brethren to form settlements in any part of the dominions of Saxony.[1] Another happy turn of events was that a little earlier than this, in 1746, the estate of Great Hennersdorf, which had belonged to the count's late grandmother, and where he had been brought up, was offered to him to purchase. As he was not then allowed to live in the country, he consented that his daughter should make the purchase.[2]

Scarcely had these favourable events taken place in England and Saxony, than the storm broke over Herrnhaag. The House of Buedingen became hostile, and required of the Brethren certain conditions with which they could not comply. The count endeavoured to compose matters, with the result that in February, 1748, it was agreed that affairs should be left in the *status quo* for the space of five years. But the situation became more serious on the accession of count Gustavus Frederic of Buedingen, when the Brethren were called upon to do homage, and at the same time it was demanded that they should renounce their elders and leaders, and particularly count Zinzendorf. The count saw that his expulsion was intended, and offered to remove the inhabitants gradually to other places, during the three years which still remained of the contract. The proposals were declined, and an order was sent to the Brethren to renounce their connection with the count. This the Brethren refused to do, and prepared to emigrate.

Ninety single men made the beginning, and went to Pennsylvania. The rest moved by degrees to other congregations in Saxony, Silesia, Holland etc. The children's institutions were transplanted chiefly to the countess Zinzendorf's estates in Upper Lusatia. Only one person is said to have renounced the ministers of the Moravian Congregation, and he soon repented, asked the Brethren's pardon, and went to live under another

[1] Cf. Bost, op. cit. p. 408.
[2] Cf. Cranz, op. cit. p. 337.

government. For a considerable time following the emigration, which was completed about 1750, the houses at Herrnhaag, for the most part, stood empty, despite attempts that were made to persuade other people to occupy them.[1]

While these events were taking place Zinzendorf continued to reside in England, where he purchased Lindsay House, on the banks of the Thames at Chelsea, from the duke of Ancaster.[2] From 1753 onwards this became the headquarters of the Moravian Church in England. The closing down of the settlement at Herrnhaag caused much loss. The year 1753 was a time of great trial. The financial affairs of the Brethren in Wetteravia, Holland and England had become complicated.[3] Spangenberg, Zinzendorf's biographer, admits that the count was defective in a clear and thorough insight into the circumstances of human life. He had no knowledge of mercantile affairs. He himself lived sparingly, but he did not possess the art of being economical, and yet in want of nothing, though the countess did.[4] The count and his wife spent the whole of their splendid incomes on the Church. Other Brethren who possessed property co-operated. But as the expense increased the count found it necessary to mortgage his estates. During his exile, however, certain of the mortgagees called in their money. Thereupon some friends in Holland advanced the sums required. This brought a temporary relief. At last one of the creditors, having fallen into difficulties, required payment; others likewise pressed for a settlement.

In England the financial affairs of the Brethren attracted much attention; particularly among the followers of Wesley and Whitefield. The expenses involved by the purchase or lease and occupation of Lindsay House seemed to them extravagant. The remarks of Wesley and Whitefield upon the situation as it became known were very severe. In this connection Tyerman speaks of 'disgrace', 'scandal' and 'inextric-

[1] Cf. Spangenberg, op. cit. pp. 396ff.; Cranz, op. cit. pp. 358ff.

[2] According to Benham, *Memoirs of Hutton*, the property was leased for 99 years, to obviate legal difficulties with regard to property held by foreigners.

[3] Cf. The long account given by Cranz, op. cit. pp. 406ff., 416.

[4] Cf. Spangenberg, op. cit. p. 400.

able confusion.' Whitefield wrote a pamphlet on the subject.[1]

Peter Boehler, who was in London at the time, did his utmost to straighten things out. The greatest assistance probably came from Frederick Köber. He was a keen business man, of iron character and tough will. He proposed the adoption of a number of measures which changed the situation. He separated the property of Zinzendorf from the general property of the Church, and put the general property under the care of a 'College of Directors.' He made arrangements whereby the 'College' should pay off all debts in fixed yearly sums. He also proposed that all members of the Church should pay a fixed annual sum to general church funds. As a natural consequence of these measures he laid it down that all members of the Church should have the right to send representatives to the General Conference. In this way he drew the outlines of the Moravian Church constitution.[2]

Zinzendorf expressed his deep sense of humiliation and regret at the situation which had developed; and made himself responsible for the whole sum in question. After things had been straightened out, the 23rd of February, 1754, was observed as a day of public thanksgiving.[3]

The community at Herrnhut had suffered a great loss in 1751 by the death of Christian David, its founder, and one of its first elders. With good reason the count thought very highly of him, and was wont to say, 'There is only one Christian David.' Now, in 1756, following quickly upon the troubles that have been indicated, the count and the whole Moravian Church, sustained another severe blow through the death of countess Zinzendorf, in the fifty-sixth year of her age. All the evidence available shows her to have been a woman of powerful and well-cultivated mind. From the beginning of their married life she shared to the full all the work which the count felt himself called to undertake. She was a woman of unaffected piety and great generosity and counted it a joy to suffer persecution and exile when the count relinquished wealth and wordly honour for the sake of his religious work.

---

[1] Cf. *The Life and Times of John Wesley*, Vol. ii. pp. 155f.
[2] Cf. Hutton, op. cit. p. 229.
[3] Cf. Bost, op. cit. pp. 410f.; Cranz, op. cit. pp. 412f., 415.

She assumed heavy responsibility in the management of both his temporal estates and his various religious establishments.[1]

The following year the count married again; this time Anna Nitschmann, one of the leading workers in the colony at Herrnhut.[2]

For the last three years of his life Zinzendorf lived at Bertholdsdorf and Herrnhut. His time was largely spent in revising his various publications.[3] His incessant labours had impaired his health, and he was ready to go when the call came. 'It will be better when I go home,' he said, 'the Conference will stand for ever.' Often during these last days he spoke to the Brethren about him on the fulfilment of our Lord's Prayer: 'That they all may be one' (John xvii 2).

Nearly a hundred people were present when he breathed his last on May 9th, 1760. He was buried in 'God's acre' at Herrnhut. Four thousand people, it is said, attended his funeral. On the simple stone that marks his grave are inscribed the words, 'He was appointed to bring forth fruit, and his fruit remains.'[4]

By all accounts Zinzendorf was an extraordinary man. From his earliest days he was deeply religious. Before his contact with the Moravian Brethren he had shown his earnest desire to devote himself to the service of Christ's Church and Kingdom. Soon after the founding of the settlement at Herrnhut he began to devote his time and strength, and his wealth, to the building up of the colony and its various extensions. As Wesley intended his United Societies to remain within the Church of England, so did Zinzendorf at first intend that the Church of the Moravian Brethren should remain within the Lutheran Church: 'A Church within a Church,' as he expressed it. But the facts were too stubborn for him, as they were for Wesley. Those who were mainly responsible for the establishment of the colony at Herrnhut remembered the Ancient Church of their fathers, and demanded that it should be reconstituted; and the count felt it to be God's will that he should assist them in this work.

[1] Ibid. pp. 410f.; Cranz, op. cit. p. 455.
[2] Cf. Spangenberg, op. cit. pp. 470f.
[3] Cf. Cranz, op. cit. pp. 448ff., 460.
[4] Cf. Hutton, op. cit. pp. 229ff.; Bost, op. cit. pp. 412f.; Spangenberg, op. cit. p. 503.

Zinzendorf has often been spoken of as the founder of the Church of the United Brethren. The facts which have been indicated in our earlier chapters show that this was not the case. The Church existed long before his birth. But its members had been dispersed and almost, as it seemed, beaten out of existence. In the work of rebuilding it the count, as we have shown, rendered the most valuable assistance. It was natural and inevitable that in the process of rebuilding many of his ideas should find expression. It is evident that his powerful personality diffused an atmosphere which pervaded most of the operations and institutions of the Church.

Mention has been made of the count's facility in poetic composition. As the years passed, he produced hymns which have won a permanent place in Christian hymnology. Numbers of them were translated by John Wesley, and are still in frequent use among the Methodists. It is difficult to imagine that the time will ever come when they will cease to be sung. Long before the Wesleys taught their followers to express their faith and experience in song, the Moravian community was already 'a nest of singing birds.' They issued the first hymn-book in 1501.

Some of the weaknesses in the character of Zinzendorf have already been mentioned. His use of sentimental language was unpleasing. A tendency to pompousness was also pointed out by his critics. The use of his many titles, and of inflated language, especially when writing to prominent individuals, invited playful, if not harsh, criticism. We have an illustration of this in a letter addressed by Zinzendorf to the Archbishop of Canterbury, which is printed by Tyerman.[1]

Such language is in striking contrast to the spartan simplicity of John Wesley. It may be accounted for partly as a result of his many associations with the crowned heads and nobility of his own and other countries, and, partly, from his desire to win recognition for the Church of the Brethren by the major branches of the Christian Church after many years of persecution, contempt and repression.

---

[1] Cf. *The Life and Times of Wesley*, Vol. ii. p. 88. See also pp. 99, 221.

CHAPTER NINETEEN

Events Following upon the Death of Zinzendorf

THE death of count Zinzendorf naturally created certain difficulties for the Church of the Brethren, particularly those of a financial character. But the Brethren continued their work, both at home and overseas. Before his death it had been decided not to hold a Synod until conditions had become more peaceful. This Synod was eventually opened at Marienborn on the first of July, 1764. Deputies were present from all parts of the world, making a total of ninety-four persons. Important matters were to be discussed, particularly with regard to the form which the Church should now assume; whether it was to be a loose body of Christian workers. or a firm, united, independent Church.[1]

The work carried on by the Brethren in all parts of the world was carefully considered. The doctrine of the Unity of the Brethren was re-affirmed to be thoroughly evangelical, its foundation being the merits of the life and sufferings of Jesus as revealed in the Scriptures and expressed in the Augsburg Confession. Attention was also given to the form of the government of the Church. A 'Directory' was chosen to have the care of the whole Unity of the Brethren in inward and outward matters. A Board of Wardens was to have the oversight of all the outward affairs of all the Congregations, and a Board of Syndics was to see that all things were done decently and in order. Count Henry Reuss was appointed to the office of the advocate of the Brethren. Other appointments were made including that of deacons.[2]

It was agreed that all Congregations and their members, wherever situated, and however diverse, should regard themselves as belonging to one Unity of Brethren. All power to

[1] Cf. Hutton, op. cit. p. 235; Cranz, op. cit. pp. 554ff.
[2] Cf. Cranz, op. cit. pp. 558f.

make laws was to be in the hands of the Synods, which were composed of all ministers of the Church and of one elected deputy from each Congregation. These Synods chose a governing body which, a little later, received the name of 'Unity Elders' Conference' (U.E.C.).[1]

In the realm of finance a rather curious experiment was made. The scheme of Köber, mentioned above, was given up. It was decided that all the property of the Church should be divided into as many sections as there were Congregations, and that each Congregation should bear its own burdens, including the maintenance of the minister. Money for general work, for example, for missions, was to be specially subscribed by the members. The machinery, however, did not work satisfactorily. In the difficult situation which followed, the single Sisters at Herrnhut set an example of sacrificial giving, and at the next Synod it was laid down that each Congregation must contribute a fixed amount towards a general fund; the U.E.C. having the oversight of every settlement.[2]

Another Synod of the Brethren was held at Marienborn in July, 1769, and was attended by one hundred and twenty-nine persons out of all the Congregations. The inward and outward state of the whole Unity of the Brethren was again carefully examined, and deep satisfaction was expressed at their unity with other Protestant Communions.

The latter half of the eighteenth century was a time of war, both in Europe and America. The conditions prevailing on the Continent gravely affected the work done by the Brethren. So early in the century as 1740 Marienborn was filled with English, Austrian and French troops. There were further outbreaks of war in 1750, 1756, and 1760. All these affected the Congregations in Germany and America, and caused much loss and damage to the settlements. Sometimes buildings were used for hospitals or for the quarterings of troops. But despite the marchings of large or small armies through the settlements and the surrounding districts, the Congregations continued their usual meetings as far as this was possible.[3]

---

[1] Cf. Cranz, op. cit. p. 620; Bost op. cit. p. 418.
[2] Cf. Hutton, op. cit. pp. 236f.
[3] Cf. Cranz, op. cit. pp. 305ff., 457, 512ff., 521ff; Spangenberg, op. cit. pp. 464ff.

Still more threatening to the spiritual life of the Brethren was the growth of Rationalism during the same period. This of course affected all the Churches. Theological students going to the seminaries or universities became imbued with the spirit of rationalistic philosophy. The works of such famous philosophers as Kant, Fichte and Jacobi displaced the Bible as the most important subject of study. The pulpits were used for the presentation of philosophical and theological essays, far above the understanding of the listeners, instead of warm-hearted Gospel messages. This new trend of things was first felt in the Brethren's theological seminary at Niesky. Till now this had been united with the Pedagogium—i.e. the college where young men received a classical education previous to beginning the study of theology proper.

Fortunately, the leaders of the Church soon perceived how fatal this new tendency would be to their own particular form of Church life, based, as it was, upon a deeply spiritual, rather emotional, type of Christian fellowship, and upon the centrality of Jesus in all their teaching and preaching. They therefore took steps to recall the people, and particularly the students, to the old paths.

One step taken was to remove the seminary from Niesky to Gnadenfeld. It was placed under the care of John Pitt, who once more gave the teaching of the Bible the central place in the curriculum, and also introduced the students to the study of the history of the Unity of the Brethren. Another step was to appoint special hours for Bible study in their settlements, and to establish monthly prayer-meetings.

Other things that helped to restore the spiritual vitality of the Church were the publication of a revised edition of the Moravian hymn-book, and the issuing by Spangenberg, in 1778, of a *Manual of Doctrine*, and, in the same year, his *Idea of the Faith of the Brethren*. The latter work became famous. For many years Spangenberg was the president of the U.E.C., and in this capacity he wielded a great influence. A worthy tribute to the contribution made by the Brethren to the spiritual recovery of the German Churches as a whole was paid by the well-known theologian Dr. Dörner, when he said, 'When the Churches were sunk in sleep, when darkness was almost everywhere, it was she, the humble priestess of the sanctuary, who fed the sacred flame.'[1]

One of the most pleasing and fruitful aspects of all the work done by the Church of the Brethren, from its early days onwards, was the care taken of the spiritual well-being and education of the children. Notice has already been taken of the fact that count Zinzendorf, as a very young child, was intensely religious. He seems never to have lost the childlike spirit, and his sense of the great importance of early religious teachings. In the arrangements he made at Herrnhut and elsewhere the religious training of the children always had a definite place. Among the various groups, called 'choirs', into which a Brethren's settlement was divided, children's choirs of boys and girls always had a place. Many references are found in the literature of the movement to the time spent by Zinzendorf himself in catechising the children and in teaching them to sing.

Love of education, and enthusiasm for it, was a legacy from the earliest days of the Unity. It resulted in the establishment of many schools, both day-schools and boarding-schools. Many of the latter became famous. It is appropriate to mention this subject here because in the work of spiritual recovery of which we are speaking, a part was played by the Pedagogium at Niesky. Somewhat later, about 1841, a spirit of concern arose among the boys, which resulted in the organization of meetings for prayer and the discussion of religious subjects. Studies, however, were in no way neglected. The boys became models of industry and decent behaviour. The life of the Church was thereby permanently enriched.[2]

During this period considerable developments were taking place in England and Ireland. After about thirty years' toil there were four main areas in which the work of the Brethren was carried on, namely, in the North, the West, the East of England, and in Ireland. In all these districts the Moravian Congregations were the centres of earnest evangelistic work. They nearly all had the various institutions which we have seen at

[1] Cf. Hutton, op. cit. p. 240; Hassé, Art. "The Moravians" in the *E. R. E.*, Vol. viii. p. 839a.
[2] Ibid. pp. 248ff.

Herrnhut, though on a smaller scale. Surrounding the main centres there were many preaching-places and small societies. After the death of Zinzendorf, Boehler and the other early leaders, Benjamin La Trobe came steadily to the front. We have seen how he became associated with John Cennick in Ireland. Thence he passed to Fulneck in Yorkshire, and became its minister. His influence, however, extended throughout the Church of the Brethren, and even beyond. He became the president of the Brethren's 'Society for the Furtherance of the Gospel,' and retained the position for life. He was in close association with the leaders of other religious Communions, including a number of bishops. He helped to heal the quarrel between the Methodists and Moravians. At the time of his death, the *London Chronicle* said of him that, 'In a variety of publications he removed every aspersion against the Brethren, and firmly established their reputation.'[1]

In a number of ways Benjamin La Trobe shared the ideas of Zinzendorf as to the way in which the Brethren should carry on their work. He clung to the idea of the Unity of the Brethren being 'A Church within a Church.' To prevent any dispute with the Church of England, he introduced a system called the 'United Flocks.' This meant that the Brethren established preaching-places without any idea of turning them into Congregations (in the Brethren's sense of this word). A strict rule was laid down that only such members of these societies as had a distinct call to join the Brethren's Church should be allowed to do so. The distinct call came through the use of the Lot. All other persons, though connected with the Brethren in a loose way, remained members of the Church of England. Once a quarter, along with a Moravian minister, they went in procession to the parish church for Holy Communion. Thus, during this period, preaching-places were maintained which had no organic connection with the Church of the Brethren.

One can hardly help but admire and appreciate the spirit of unity, and the humble-mindedness, which led the Brethren at this time to become hand-maidens, so to speak, to the Church of England. Whether, however, this mode of operation was wise and helpful from their own point of view—of build-

---

[1] Ibid. p. 254.

ing up an independent, self-governing Church—may be questioned. Hutton is probably right in his view that the adoption of this mode of operation is largely accountable for the failure of many preaching-places to establish themselves as local Churches. The system of 'United Flocks,' he says, was all right on paper. It showed a brotherly spirit and a love of unity. But Englishmen have never been fond of half and half notions. It might, he remarks, do well in Germany; but it did not succeed here. Had the Brethren gone boldly forward, like the Independents or the Wesleyans, the story might have been very different.[1]

But there were other factors operative during the first half of the nineteenth century which were partly responsible for the slowing down of the movement. The building of the railways made it easier for townspeople and the villagers to travel from place to place. In the early days, the settlements were to a great extent isolated communities. They created a fellowship that was attractive; the like of which was to be found nowhere else. They had their own industries and other occupations. It was convenient and helpful to live in such warm-hearted communities. But better transport, by road and rail, changed the relations between the settlements and the rest of the population. People now sought work elsewhere. The choir-meetings, band-meetings, prayer-meetings, and other fellowships, declined. At last only four settlements proper remained in England and Ireland, namely, Fulneck, Fairfield, Ockbrook and Gracehill.[2]

A change in the situation came about 1850. The rule that no member should publish a book or pamphlet without the permission of the Church was repealed; and a magazine, entitled 'The Fraternal Messenger,' was begun, and called aloud for revival. Fresh ideas were put forth. A Synod was held, and for the first time the Brethren called themselves no longer a 'Unity' merely but a Church. They realized now, more keenly than previously that the people of England were still largely unchristian. A Home Mission Association was established, followed by county or district Associations. Regular Congrega-

[1] Cf. op. cit. pp. 256ff., 263.
[2] Ibid. pp. 262f.

K

tions were formed; open-air preaching was commenced, and various other forms of evangelism were introduced. All these activities were under the supervision of the Provincial Elders' Conference. The Brethren adopted methods of work which were familiar in other branches of the Church. Brethren's Houses and Sisters' Houses were displaced in favour of such things as Young Men's Associations and Juvenile Missionary Associations.

All these things meant that the Church of the Brethren, whilst retaining the fundamental forms of its life was prepared to adapt itself to the changed intellectual and social environment, and to carry on its work as an independent Church, discharging what it believed to be its God-given task.

CHAPTER TWENTY

The Early Missions of the Brethren

SEVERAL references have been made in an earlier chapter to the various missions which were undertaken by the Moravians at a time when they were still a very small and struggling community.[1] Since, however, interest in aggressive missionary work, particularly among people in difficult and dangerous situations, has been so dominant a feature of Moravian Church life, I wish to indicate in a little more detail the nature of their work. A brief summary only can be attempted. Anything like a full account would require far more space than can here be allotted.

It has been observed that interest in mission work in the West Indies began during a visit paid by Zinzendorf to the court of Denmark in 1731, in order to attend the coronation of King Christian VI. Some of the Brethren who attended him on this occasion became acquainted with a Negro from the West Indies, named Anthony, who was then in the employ of a Dutch nobleman. The Negro described the miserable condition of the Negroes in the island of St. Thomas, and told of the longing of many, and especially of his own sister, to be made acquainted with the way of salvation. The story which he heard at this time made a deep impression upon the count, and on his return to Herrnhut he reported on what he had heard to the Brethren.[2]

The account thus given created in the minds of two young men, Leonard Dober and Tobias Leupold, an eager desire to go and carry the Gospel to the Negroes, a desire which was intensified when Anthony, the Negro referred to, was allowed to visit Herrnhut and to give his own account to the Brethren. He explained that there would be scarcely any opportunity for missionaries to instruct the Negroes unless they became as

---

[1] Cf. *supra*, pp. 78, 86, 116.
[2] Cf. Cranz, op. cit. pp. 148ff.; Hutton, op. cit. p. 150; Spangenberg, op. cit. pp. 143f.

slaves. As the Negroes were overwhelmed with work, there was no chance to speak to them except during the hours of labour. The two young men remained undaunted by the picture of the harsh life that awaited them if they still carried out their design. They declared their readiness to sell themselves into slavery and to sacrifice their lives in order to gain even a single soul for Christ.

But there were other difficulties to be overcome. At first the Church generally did not favour the design, regarding it as a well-intentioned but impracticable enterprise. Martin Linner, the chief elder, who was the superintendent of the choir of single Brethren, refused to consent to part with Dober, who was very useful in that branch of the activity of the Church. He had, in fact, fixed on Dober as the person best fitted to succeed him in his important office, which he felt he would soon be compelled to relinquish on the ground of failing health.[1]

A year passed away before the matter was finally decided by the Church. The case of Leupold was then submitted to the decision of the Lot, which indicated that he ought not to go for the present. But Dober still persisted in his intention. Then the count, who himself sympathised with his design, asked him if he too would submit himself to the same decision. He replied that as to the conviction of his own mind there was no necessity, but for the satisfaction of the Brethren they might do as they wished. They then followed the usual procedure, and asked him to draw one from a number of slips of paper, on which different sentences had been written; he drew the slip which contained the words, 'Let the youth go, for the Lord is with him.' Thus the issue was decided. Dober received the appointment, and Linner gave him his blessing in the name of the Church. As Dober did not wish to go alone, he asked them to give him David Nitschmann for a companion, at least till the mission was established. Nitschmann immediately agreed to the proposal, though it meant leaving his wife and children in Europe.[2]

On the 18th of August, 1732, the two missionaries took leave

---

[1] Cf. Bost, op. cit. p. 276.
[2] Cf. Hutton, op. cit. p. 150.

of the Church, and left Herrnhut on the 21st. Zinzendorf gave each of them a ducat (about half a guinea) in addition to three dollars which they had received from the Church; and thus equipped they set off on the journey to Copenhagen, a distance of some 120 leagues. On the way, they visited several pious persons and explained their design. Only one of these, the countess of Stollberg, encouraged them to persevere. Everywhere they were told of difficulties and dangers, arising from the unhealthy climate and the degraded condition of the Negroes. Undeterred, however, they pursued their way.

On their arrival at Copenhagen they were confronted with the same discouragements. Persons of all ranks declared their mission to be impossible of achievement. All sorts of objections were raised. The directors of the West India Company, it was said, would oppose their project; the condition of the natives was such that they could not appreciate their message; in reply to their assertion that they would work as slaves, it was affirmed that they would not be allowed to do this. When Nitschmann declared that he would work as a carpenter, the objectors said, 'But what will this man, the potter (Dober) do?' 'I will support him by my work,' replied Nitschmann.

When it was found that by no argument or opposition could the would-be missionaries be prevented from pursuing their cherished design, there was some reaction in their favour. Two court chaplains, convinced that the project was in accordance with God's purpose, brought others to the same view. The royal family having been informed of their design, the Queen was disposed to favour them, and one of the princesses sent them a sum of money for their voyage, and presented them with a Dutch Bible. Several other persons, including a number of Counsellors of State, gave them similar tokens of regard.

As none of the West India Company's vessels would take them on board, one of the King's officers helped them to procure a passage in a Dutch ship, bound for St. Thomas. The kindness of their friends enabled them, not only to pay their passage, but also to furnish themselves with carpenter's tools for the use of Nitschmann. The missionaries embarked on the 8th of October, 1732, and the vessel set sail the next day.[1]

[1] Cf. Bost, op. cit. pp. 278f.

The voyage, which was often performed in three or four weeks, lasted ten, and was accomplished with much danger and inconvenience. The missionaries arrived at St. Thomas on December 13th. Immediately on their arrivel a Negro came to invite them to the house of a Mr. Lorenzen, a planter, whose sister in Copenhagen had given them a letter of recommendation, and had also furnished them with other introductions. Until they could procure a residence for themselves, Mr. Lorenzen offered them board and lodging in his own house. They began their labours on the same day. For a time, David Nitschmann, working as a carpenter, earned their livelihood.

On the afternoon of their arrival they went to see Anthony's sister, and also a brother, who gladly welcomed them as teachers sent from God. The two missionaries sought every opportunity of conversing with the Negroes, visiting them on Saturdays and Sundays. The latter were very appreciative, for never before had they been treated with so much kindness. The white people, however, were divided in their opinion. Some honoured them as servants of God. Others despised them as deceivers of the people and were minded to drive them out of the country.

Nitschmann had little difficulty in finding sufficient work to maintain himself and his companion. It should be remembered, however, that he had only made the journey as a companion to Dober, in order to assist him in initiating the work, and had been charged to return as soon as possible.[1] Dober therefore was anxious to find some means of gaining a living by his trade as a potter. This proved to be impossible, both on account of the bad quality of the clay, and because there was no proper kiln. Some other means of earning a livelihood had therefore to be found. Despite the difficulty of the situation he readily agreed that Nitschmann should return home on the date fixed, namely, in April, 1733. He did so, and arrived at Herrnhut on July 24th, after an absence of eleven months.

Within three weeks of being left alone Dober received a proposal from the governor (Gardelin) to become steward of his household. He accepted the appointment on the condition that he should have liberty, after he had finished his business, to

[1] Cf. Bost, op. cit. p. 281; Cranz, op. cit. p. 185.

attend to the Negroes. But though he now had everything he could wish in a material sense, he soon became dissatisfied because he felt that his missionary work was being prejudiced. He therefore relinquished his post with the governor, hired a room for himself, and endeavoured to get his living by watching the plantations or by other labour of a like nature. Thus he lived in great poverty; but now, as he said, he was like a bird which had recovered its liberty. He was free to give himself wholly to winning the natives.

After some ten months, in 1734, a ship arrived bringing welcome reinforcements. His friend Leupold and two other Brethren, Schenk and Miksch, arrived bringing the glad news that eighteen persons—fourteen Brethren and four Sisters—had come with them to form a colony at St. Croix, where there were plantations belonging to De Pless, the King of Denmark's chamberlain.[1] But they also brought news of Dober's recall, as he had been chosen elder of the Church at Herrnhut, in the place of Martin Linner who had passed away. Dober embarked on April 12th to return on the same vessel which had brought the eighteen colonists for St. Croix. He took with him a young Negro, seven years old, the first-fruits of the Brethren's work among the heathen. Dober reached Herrnhut in February, 1735. During the two years he had spent at St. Thomas he had the pleasure of seeing four Negroes receive the Gospel; and others were inclined to do so and were afterwards converted.[2]

Such were the small beginnings of the great work which was later to be done by the Brethren overseas. Dober was succeeded by Frederic Martin. He was accompanied by a Dr. Grotthaus, a celebrated physician from Copenhagen, who was impelled to share the enterprise by learning of the many Brethren who had died of sickness at St. Croix. He died soon after his arrival. Within a few years hundreds of people had responded to the call of the Gospel preached by Martin and his assistants. As none of the missionaries had been ordained before they went abroad, they were not allowed to administer baptism; but Martin received ordination afterwards in writing. The fruits of the

---

[1] Cf. Hutton, op. cit. p. 152; Spangenberg, op. cit. pp. 174f.
[2] Cf. Cranz, op. cit. pp. 185ff.; Bost, op. cit. pp. 288ff.

mission in St. Thomas were baptized by Spangenberg during his visit there in 1736.[1]

The beginning of the Brethren's work in Greenland was equally adventurous, but of this also I shall speak only briefly. Its origin must be traced back to the same visit to Denmark paid by Zinzendorf in 1731 to which I have referred, and which led to the West Indian mission. Whilst at Copenhagen Zinzendorf made the acquaintance of two baptized Greenlanders, and also learned much concerning the work of a Danish missionary named Egède. The count was grieved to learn that it was doubtful whether the mission could be continued. He thereupon resolved, if possible, to send this missionary some assistance. When the matter was discussed at Herrnhut two of the Brethren, Matthew Stach and Fr. Böenisch, expressed a desire to share in this enterprise. Their desire was communicated to the Church, but so obvious were the difficulties and dangers involved in a mission in such a cold and remote part of the world that the Church delayed to give a decision for more than a year.

When at length the Church decided to give its blessing to the enterprise, as Böenisch was engaged on another journey, Christian David offered to accompany the mission, and Matthew Stach chose his cousin, Christian Stach, for his companion. Only two days' notice was given of their departure; but their preparations were soon completed, since they took nothing with them except their clothes. They trusted to Providence to supply their needs. Their expenses on the road were defrayed by a small sum of money presented to them by the Church, being part of a donation which had just been received from a friend in Venice. They were set apart for the work by the elder Augustin Neisser, by prayer and imposition of hands. They left Herrnhut on January 19th, 1733, five months after the departure of Nitschmann and Dober for St. Thomas.[2]

On their arrival at Copenhagen they received a kindly welcome from the friends to whom they had been recommended. But the situation was heavy with discouragement. It was actually being debated whether all communications with Green-

[1] Cf. Cranz, op. cit. p. 186; Spangenberg, op. cit. p. 226.
[2] Cf. Bost, op. cit. pp. 285ff.; Spangenberg, op. cit. pp. 166f.

land should be broken off, and whether the vessel which was about to be sent out should bring back the persons stationed there, both those employed in trade and those in the mission. The missionaries were told that they would perish of cold and hunger or be killed by the savages. They remained unmoved by these gloomy prognostications. And having learned that the King had consented to the fitting out of a vessel for the Danish colony at Goodhaab, they obtained leave, through De Pless, to embark in her, the King writing with his own hand to Egède, to recommend them to his care.

De Pless also showed them great kindness, after setting clearly before them the many difficulties and dangers of the enterprise. He introduced them to persons of high rank and devoted piety; and these encouraged them to proceed, and also furnished them with resources sufficient to defray the expenses of their voyage and settlement in Greenland. As no timber was available on the spot, they had to take sufficient wood with them with which to build a house, as well as such materials and tools as were necessary for this purpose. These, and many other things in addition, were provided by the friends at Copenhagen. The missionaries set sail from Copenhagen on April 10th, 1733. After a prosperous voyage they arrived in Davis's Strait in the beginning of May. At this point their progress was arrested by a storm which lasted four days. On the 20th of May, however, they arrived at Ball's River after a voyage of six weeks, near the place where they afterwards established the settlement called New Herrnhut.[1]

On their arrival they were kindly received by Egède, who offered to assist them in learning the language. Speedily they set to work to build a hut, in the Greenland fashion, of stones, with turfs laid between them. Though it was now June, the cold was so intense that the turfs often froze in their hands. By June 6th their cabin was so far completed that they could enter it, which they did with thanksgiving.

In August, 1734, two assistants, Böenisch and John Beck, arrived. As Christian David had only been sent out to accompany his Brethren and to help in the first arrangements, he began to make preparations for his return.

[1] Cf. Bost, op. cit. p. 288.

The year 1735 was one of extreme difficulty. Food was scarce. There was much sickness. Smallpox ravaged the community, brought by a Greenlander boy who had been to Copenhagen. It was the first time the dread disease had ever been known there. The previous year they had been supplied with provisions by a friend at court. This year they seemed to be entirely forgotten. They had not asked the assistance of the Church at Herrnhut, who, for lack of experience, knew not how to help them. Their whole provision for the year consisted of a cask and a half of oatmeal, half a cask of peas, and six barrels of biscuits. The Danish colonists could offer little assistance, because their own supplies also were exhausted. The missionaries understood nothing about catching seals, which were the principal resource of the country. The Greenlanders were not yet friendly, and though they knew their distress they would only sell to them at extravagant prices. Often the missionaries were driven to appease their hunger with shell-fish and raw sea-weed.[1]

On the return of Christian David, the Brethren had requested the Church at Herrnhut to send out some of the Sisters, who might help them in their domestic concerns, so as to enable them to devote themselves more freely to their mission work. In response to their appeal, in 1736, the Church sent them the widow Stach, Matthew's mother, with her two daughters and a brother, who engaged to conduct them to Greenland. The same vessel which brought them, took back the aged Egède, exhausted with the labours of fifteen years. Christian Stach also returned by the same vessel, in order to give the Church an account of the progress and needs of the mission. When the same vessel returned it brought them all necessary supplies, and continued from that time to make regular voyages with provisions.[2]

These early years were apparently fruitless. The Greenlanders who came from a distance were dull of apprehension, and soon forgot the teaching given them. Those near by, at Ball's River, seemed to grow worse rather than better. But in 1738 a change became noticeable. In June of that year a group

[1] Cf. Bost, op. cit. p. 293; Hutton, op. cit. pp. 154f.
[2] Ibid. p. 294.

of Greenlanders came to see the missionaries. Beck gave them an account of the coming of Jesus to redeem men, and described His sufferings and death. The heart of one of the savages, called Kajarnak, who had not heard the Gospel before, was deeply moved. He cried out that he too wished to be saved. Beck again repeated the Gospel story, and soon others in the group were expressing amazement at what they heard. When they left they promised to return.

From that time Kajarnak, particularly, visited the missionaries frequently, and at length came to live near them. He proved to be intelligent, appreciative and capable of understanding the truths of the Gospel. He fetched his family and others, who lived with him in the same tent, nine persons in all, and several others followed him. The Brethren established a daily prayer-meeting for the adults, a school for the children, and another meeting for instruction with a view to baptism. During the same period the missionaries continued to visit natives scattered along the coast.

In the beginning of 1739 there was an extremely severe frost, and, in consequence, so great a famine that several natives died of cold and hunger. Many of them sought refuge with the missionaries, whose two houses were so crowded that there was scarcely room to move. Fifteen or twenty Greenlanders were provided with meals each day. Kajarnak assisted in this work with great zeal. The missionaries seized this opportunity of setting forth Jesus to the people as the true Bread of Life. When they returned to their homes in the spring several of the natives carried with them impressions which bore good fruit later on.

On Easter Sunday of that year Kajarnak and three members of his family received Christian baptism—the first-fruits of the mission to Greenland. The four baptized persons were given new names; Kajarnak was called Samuel.[1]

Persecution, however, was not lacking in these early days. Enemies plotted the death of Kajarnak. Already they had murdered his brother-in-law; and he had to flee south to preserve his life. To the great joy of the Brethren, however, he returned a year later and presented himself at one of their love-feasts.

[1] Cf. Bost, op. cit. pp. 296ff.

He brought with him numerous Greenlanders to whom he had preached the Gospel during his flight.

A few years later a great awakening took place among the Greenlanders. The seekers increased to such a degree that in 1758 the Congregation amounted to four hundred baptized persons. A second Congregation was formed at Lichtenfeld, in the Fisher's Bay. This was still flourishing when Cranz wrote his *History of Greenland* in 1765.[1]

Shortly after the beginnings of the missions to the West Indies and Greenland an attempt was made to begin a similar work in Lapland. It was the custom at Herrnhut to read reports of the progress of the Kingdom of Christ in various parts of the world to the members of the Congregation. In 1734, after such accounts had been read to the Brethren, three of their number, namely, Andrew Grasmann, Daniel Schneider and John Nitschmann, offered to carry the Gospel to Lapland. Their offer was looked upon with favour by the Church; but they were instructed not to go to those parts where other missionaries were already at work, but only to those which had not yet been visited. In May of that year the missionaries travelled to Stockholm, where they learned the language. In 1735 they travelled to Tornea in Lapland; and having learned the language of that part they travelled through all Swedish Lapland. Finding, however, that preparations were already in hand for the conversion of those peoples they resolved to go to Russian Lapland. Before doing so, in 1736, Andrew Grasmann and Daniel Schneider returned to Stockholm, where they found Michael Miksch, who had come to take the place of John Nitschmann, who had returned to Herrnhut in 1735. In the beginning of the year 1737 the three Brethren met in Reval, and travelled together to Moscow and Archangel. There they became acquainted with some Samojedes, who were willing to take them with them.

Difficulties, however, were now encountered. On applying for a passport they were arrested on suspicion of being Swedish spies. For a time they were kept in separate places of confinement; and after five weeks they were taken to St. Petersburg. At first their guards treated them with great severity. But one

[1] Cf. Cranz, op. cit. pp. 187, 391, 488; See also Spangenberg, op. cit. pp. 486f.

day, when crossing a lake during a thaw, the ice broke, and two of the soldiers and two of the Brethren fell into the water. The third missionary helped them out again, after which experience they were treated with greater kindness.

On reaching St. Petersburg they were again imprisoned for five weeks and frequently examined. Eventually a minister of the crown, being convinced of their innocence, furnished them with a passport to Lubec, saying to them, 'Ye may go your way, good people; your service is not wanted here. Possibly the time may soon come when ye will be sent for, and then ye may come again.' Thus for the time being their mission was frustrated.[1]

A mission to the Esquimaux of the Labrador territory followed closely upon the mission to Greenland. The Brethren in Greenland formed the opinion that the Greenlanders came originally from North America, and that some of them were probably still there. They felt a desire to take the Gospel to them. Matthew Stach sought an opportunity in vain to get to Hudson's Bay. Consequently some Brethren in London, in company with a number of well-disposed merchants, decided to fit out a trading vessel for the coast of the Labrador territory. Matthew Stach having gone to Greenland again, the Brethren in London requested Zinzendorf to send other Brethren to preach the Gospel to the heathen in those parts. A Dutch mate named Christian Erhard, who had several times been in Davis's Strait on the whale fishery, and had visited New Herrnhut in Greenland, and now lived in the Brethren's Settlement at Zeist, offered to join the four Brethren who were willing to settle in the country, to learn the language, in order to evangelize the heathen.[2]

Count Zinzendorf felt some hesitation concerning this enterprise, as trading interests were involved, but was unwilling to hinder the attempt. The four Brethren involved in the enterprise took with them a house ready framed, a boat and all kinds of implements, and seeds for the cultivation of the land. They sailed from London on the 17th May, 1752, and entered a bay on the coast of Labrador on July 31st. The bay, from one of

[1] Cf. Cranz, op. cit. p. 189.
[2] Cf. Cranz, op. cit. p. 404.

the owners of the ship, received the name Nisbet's Haven. Here they resolved to settle. They called their house 'Hoffenthal', which means 'The Valley of Hope.'

On September 5th Erhard went with the ship further north for the purposes of trade. He knew something of their language, and could make himself fairly well understood by the Esquimaux. As the latter professed to be afraid to come on board, on account of the arms that were carried, Erhard was persuaded to go to them, with five other men, in an unarmed boat, to trade. From this adventure they never returned. The ship, having no other boat, could not go to seek for them, and was compelled to return to the Brethren. The captain represented to them his distress in that, having lost his best men and the boat, he was unable to navigate the ship, and desired them to return with him. They, therefore, with regret left their house, hoping to take possession of it again next year, and returned to England, arriving there about the end of November.

The count thanked God heartily for the safe return of the four Brethren. He was unwilling that they should journey thither again until a report should be received as to whether the missing men were still alive, and the house still standing. The ship sailed thither the next year, and word was brought that some bodies of the murdered persons had been found. These were buried. The house was found standing by the crew of another ship; but soon after it was reported to have been destroyed. Further attempts to evangelize these parts were for a time postponed.[1]

Another attempt, however, was made in 1764. In that year Fens Haven, one of the assistants of the mission in Greenland, saw the fulfilment of his oft-expressed wish to be allowed to undertake a mission to the Esquimaux. He was of the opinion that God had only led him to Greenland to give him the opportunity of learning the language, which was believed to be similar to that of the Esquimaux. When his place in Greenland was supplied by others he sought and obtained the consent and blessing of the Unity of the Brethren to undertake the mission. In the spring of 1764 he set out for England.

By the assistance of the Brethren in England he obtained the

---

[1] Cf. Cranz, op. cit. p. 405; Hutton, op. cit. p. 156.

permission and the patronage of the then governor of New-foundland and Labrador, Hugh Palliser, to attempt a visit. After overcoming many difficulties he at last landed on the coast of Labrador. On September 4th he discovered a number of Esqui-maux on the island of Quirpont, on the north-east point of Newfoundland. To their great wonder and delight he addressed them in their own language, which had never before been done by a European. He explained to them the intention of his voyage, to make them acquainted with their Creator by preach-ing the Gospel. They received him in the most friendly manner, and gave him a pledge of friendship. He promised to come again, with more Brethren the following year.[1]

The declaration of friendship from savages, with whom no European's life had before been safe, was agreeable to the governor, and through him to the Board of Trade and Planta-tions. For the security of trade and fishery these expressed a desire to see a mission of the Brethren established there. The next year (1765), therefore, Fens Haven, with the former Danish missionary, Christian Laurence Drachart, and two other Brethren, went thither again. This time they made a still longer journey in reconnoitring the country. But much as the Esqui-maux desired a mission to be established, as also did certain persons of rank in England, various difficulties caused it to be postponed for some time longer.

In 1768 negotiations on this matter were renewed. On the report of the Board of Trade to the Privy Council a resolution was passed on the 3rd of May, 1769, concerning the establish-ment of a mission in the Labrador territory, and on May 8th an Order in Council was issued to this effect: 'That the land desired in Esquimaux Bay should be granted to the *Unitas Fratrum* and their *Society for the Furtherance of the Gospel among the Heathen*, and that they be protected in their laud-able undertakings, etc.'

It was too late that year to put the matter into execution. But at the Synod held in 1769 it was decided that in the year 1770 another voyage should be undertaken in that region, in order to seek out a place for a building for the mission, and to renew and confirm their friendly acquaintance with the Esqui-

[1] Cf. Cranz, op. cit. p. 607.

maux. This enterprise was carried through with success. The mission to Labrador was established in 1771.

Another of the early missions of the Brethren was established in Surinam (Dutch Guiana). Spangenberg, on his journey through Holland to England (1734),[1] in order to forward the Brethren to Georgia, made inquiry concerning the state of Surinam in South America, where the Surinam Company in Holland were settling colonies, and inviting people from all countries to form them. As it was necessary to address the Company in writing, Spangenberg needed a person capable of translating the writings with which he was furnished into Low Dutch, and was directed to Isaac Lelong. This person made Spangenberg and the Congregation of the Brethren known to many clergymen and other religious persons. With these Spangenberg formed a useful acquaintance.[2]

Upon the memorial which he presented a committee of the Company was nominated with whom he treated concerning the conditions upon which the Brethren would form a settlement in Surinam. In the summer of 1735 the first three Brethren set off on their voyage thither. Their object was to obtain a more complete knowledge of the country, and especially of its heathen inhabitants. Other Brethren followed in 1738 and 1740, having obtained a grant from the directors of the Company. They purchased and cultivated a plantation, not far from Paramaribo, and laboured among the Negroes and Indians. Difficulties, however, arose, partly due to holding meetings in their own habitations, which their neighbours attended in great numbers, and partly, afterwards, to dissensions among the Brethren themselves. In 1745 they decided to leave the colony, some of them withdrawing to Pennsylvania, and others to the neighbouring Rio de Berbice.

In 1754 the Brethren were again invited to Surinam. In that year Lewis Christopher Dehne, one of the first Brethren who went to Berbice in 1738, went from Bethlehem to Paramaribo, with Mark Ralfs.[3] Working at their trades these men waited for an opening to evangelize the Indians in those parts. The

---

[1] See *supra*, p. 86.
[2] Cf. Cranz, op. cit. p. 195.
[3] Ibid. p. 484f.

former governor of Berbice, who now lived at Paramaribo, introduced them to the governor of Surinam, who expressed a desire that the Brethren would form an establishment in Surinam, offering them as much land as they would need for a colony and a mission. In consequence the missionary Schumann and Nathaniel Seidel, in 1755, set out from Berbice for Surinam to seek for a suitable tract of land, and to treat further with the governor about the settlement. Abraham Bemper, who had formerly lived in Surinam, went with them. The distance between the two places is only one hundred and sixty leagues, but the voyage was difficult because it involved travelling up and down several rivers.

First they pitched upon some suitable land on the rivers Corentyn and Sarameca, and then went on to Paramaribo. After referring the matter to the government in Holland a confirmation of the immunities granted was received in 1756. In the autumn of that year Captain Nicholas Garrison went thither with eight Brethren to take possession of the land granted on the Sarameca and the Corentyn, and to treat further with the government concerning the colony and the mission.

In the spring of 1757 five Brethren made the beginning of some buildings on the Sarameca, and called the place Sharon. In August they were visited by the missionary Schumann, from Berbice, who brought with him thirty Indians who desired to live there. By the year 1759 the Congregation had increased to sixty-two.[1]

I must not attempt to relate in detail the further developments of this mission. It was one of the most arduous and dangerous of all the missionary undertakings carried through during this period. The missionaries were exposed to constant danger from the suspicious Indians, as well as from wild beasts and venemous serpents. Once hostile Negroes raided Sharon, murdered three Indians, and carried away eleven prisoners.[2] But two of the Brethren continued to man the post despite the fact that in 1761 they were gravely ill for nearly a year. When missionaries passed away, through toiling in such grievous

[1] Cf. Cranz, op. cit. p. 486.
[2] Cf. Cranz, op. cit. pp. 487, 546; Hutton, op. cit. p. 158.

L

conditions, there were always those who willingly offered to go out and take their places.

For the rest it must suffice to say that in all the places I have mentioned—in the West Indies, in Greenland and Labrador, in Surinam—the mission work of the Moravian Church has been continued. In later years other mission stations have been begun, and are still manned with the same steadfast devotion. What Bost wrote in 1834 is still true: The history of their operations 'presents some of the noblest specimens of Christian heroism, both in action and suffering, ever recorded. The Brethren have seemed to delight in attempting what most men would have regarded as impracticable; and their perseverance has equalled their courage. . . . . . The Church of the United Brethren may indeed be called a 'Missionary Church.' No other body of professing Christians can lay an equal claim to that appellation.'[1]

[1] Cf. Bost, op. cit. p. 422. See further Hutton op. cit. pp. 158ff.; 277; also *Periodical Accounts of the Work of the Moravian Missions* 1954.

CHAPTER TWENTY-ONE

Constitutional Changes
and Other Developments

THE main features of the Church of the United Brethren as it existed during many centuries have perhaps been sufficiently indicated in our earlier chapters. It will, however, be convenient here to recall some of its leading characteristics and notice certain later developments.

From the beginning the government of the Church has been presbyterial—a government by elders—with the Synod as the supreme court. When the Brethren met in Synod at Marienborn, in 1764, they chose a Directing Board of nine Brethren, which was to have supreme authority during the period between the Synods. Ever since that time, the Unity Elders' Conference has held the reins of government. It was (and is) chosen by a Synod of the whole Church. Its functions have included the management of the finances, the arrangement of visitations, the appointment of ministers, the supervision of missions, and much other necessary work. It issues annual reports of the work of the Church. It has thus served through the years as the bond of union of the Church.[1]

The orders of the Church's ministry are bishops, presbyters and deacons. The year 1457 is usually regarded as the date of the founding of the Church. In that year, as we have seen, a group of men in Kunwald (Moravia) formed themselves into a church fellowship, and chose a number of elders to have oversight over them.[2] A few years later, in 1467, three of their elders received episcopal ordination through Stephen, bishop of the Waldenses.[3] Since that time, the episcopal succession among the Brethren has been carefully maintained. We have

[1] Cf. Hutton, op. cit. p. 267; Bost, op. cit. p. 418; Hassé, E. R. E., Vol. viii. p. 840a, b.
[2] Cf. supra, pp. 30f. Cranz, op. cit. pp. 23, 27.
[3] Cf. Cranz, op. cit. pp. 28f; and see supra, pp. 35f.

seen with what care they sought to preserve the succession of bishops after the Church was reconstituted at Herrnhut in 1722. In 1735 David Nitschmann was consecrated, at Berlin, a bishop of the Brethren's Church by bishop Daniel Ernest Jablonsky, grandson of Bishop Comenius.[1] In the administration of the Church the bishops alone have power of ordination.

We shall not here discuss the question of the validity of this succession of bishops from the point of view of the Anglican Church. By some clergy it has been recognised as a true succession; by others it has been disputed.[2] In any case, the Church of the United Brethren claims to be a genuine episcopal Church on the New Testament model.

As the Church expanded it came to include three separate branches on the Continent—in Bohemia, Moravia, and Poland; but it remained organically one. The attempts that were made by Church and State to stamp it out have been briefly described. These resulted in the foundation of a new centre at Herrnhut in Saxony. Soon other centres were established in Germany, Denmark, Holland, England, and America. The Unity of the Brethren was, in fact, the first international Protestant Church.

For nearly a century all these new developments were controlled from Germany by the Unity Elders' Conference. From time to time, as the Lot directed, a General Synod was held, in which representatives of each Congregation assembled, passed the laws of the Church, and elected the governing body to supervise and guide the affairs of the Church until the next Synod.

It was natural that, as the years passed, and the work in England and America developed, the workers in these fields should feel the need for the exercise of greater powers in the direction of their own affairs. So far, though they had been allowed to hold Conferences, they had not been allowed to make laws. Their Provincial Elders' Conferences were ap-

---

[1] See supra, pp. 87f.

[2] On this subject the student may refer to the following tracts: Report of the Committee appointed by the Archbishop of Canterbury to consider the Orders of the Unitas Fratrum or Moravians (1906); and Bishop, E. R. Hassé's, The Relation of the Moravian Church to the Church of England (Lond. 1908).

pointed by the Unity Elders' Conference. All their schools, finances, and their work in general, were practically controlled from Germany.[1]

By the middle of the nineteenth century there were some Brethren who were of the opinion that certain changes should be introduced; and that the German Province ought to have less, and the English and American Provinces more, power. These matters were brought up for discussion in a General Synod in 1857, on the initiative of the American representatives. After much discussion a new constitution, much like that which exists today, was established. According to this, the General Synod, which meets every six years, remains the supreme legislative body, and the Unity Elders' Conference the supreme administrative body. Certain changes were, however, introduced into the composition of the Synod, to make it more elective and democratic.

It was also decided that the American and British Provinces should have their own Synods—until this time they had only Conferences—and that these should have supreme legislative powers in their respective Provinces. The Provincial Synod is composed of all the ordained ministers of the Church, together with lay representatives of each Congregation. It has power to settle the time and place of its own meetings, and to elect deputies to the General Synod. Each Province was also to have power to elect a Governing Board, called a Provincial Elders' Conference, and to manage its own finances and property.

In 1879 this constitution was modified so as to place the work of Missions, regarded as a fourth Province, in which the whole Church took part, under the direction of the Unity Elder's Conference, as elected by the General Synod.[2]

Each Congregation of the Brethren manages its own affairs, subject to the general laws of the Province. In co-operation with the minister, it is the responsibility of the Church, through its Committee or Council, to watch over the welfare and discipline of its members.

In Germany, and elsewhere on the Continent, the Church of the Brethren retains certain features which have disappeared

[1] Cf. Hutton, op. cit. pp. 268f.

[2] Ibid. pp. 270f.; Hassé, E. R. E., Vol. viii. p. 838b.

from the Church in the British and American Provinces. In the settlements, for example, there are still schools, Brethren's Houses, Sisters' Houses and Diaconies. Each settlement aims to be a closely united band of earnest disciples. A special feature is the so-called Diaspora. Its object is to promote spiritual life and fellowship within the National Church by the formation of small societies within the local Churches, without, however, any intention of their becoming branches of the Brethren's Church. A synodal resolution expressly forbids any workers to proselytise. The intention is to promote the spirit of unity among the Churches, as well as the well-being of individuals.[1]

In its worship the Church combines the liturgical element with a large measure of freedom in extempore prayer. The Book of Worship includes two liturgies for public service. It contains also services for the baptism of infants, for confirmation, ordination, marriage and burial. Along with these there is a revised collection of hymns of all ages—the latest successor of the first Protestant hymn-book ever used.[2]

The belief of the Church is Trinitarian; and the main points of its doctrine are those that find expression in the Apostles' Creed, the Nicene Creed, the Augsburg and Westminster Confessions, and in the Thirty-nine Articles of the Church of England. The Holy Scriptures are held to be the only rule of faith and conduct and the final court of appeal. Difference of view is allowed in non-essentials, and more stress is laid on Christian character and life than on opinions. Ever since it separated from Rome the Church of the Brethren has sought to emphasise points of agreement with other Evangelical Churches, rather than points of difference.

The present organisation and activities of the Moravian Church may be briefly summarized as follows. Four groups are recognised. These are :

1. The 'Home' Provinces, fully self-dependent and self-governing: (a) British Province, (b) Continental Province, (c) American Province, North, (d) American Province, South.

2. The Moravian Church in Czechoslovakia, a Province in a state of transition toward full self-dependence.

---

[1] Cf. Hassé, *E. R. E.*, Vol. viii., p. 839a; Hutton, op. cit. p. 275.
[2] Ibid. p. 840a.

3. The Mission Provinces, which are in a state of transition toward self-dependence: (a) Jamaica, (b) West Indies, East, including British Guiana, (c) Surinam, (d) South Africa, West, (e) Nicaragua.

4. The Mission Fields: (a) West Himalaya, (b) Unyamwezi, (c) Southern Highlands, (d) Labrador, (e) South Africa, East, (f) Honduras, (g) Alaska, (h) California.[1]

The Congregations of the British Province are grouped in the following five Districts: (1) The Yorkshire District, (2) The Lancashire District, (3) The Eastern District, (4) The Western District, (5) The Irish District.

The list of Ministers in the British Province shows thirty-nine on the active list and eleven retired. There are 3,223 members and adherents; 2,844 teachers and scholars in the Sunday Schools, and 658 scholars in the Boarding Schools.

As already indicated, the Church in Czechoslovakia is recognised as a Province in a state of transition toward full self-dependence. It may here be added that it is recognized by the State under the name of 'Jednota Bratrska.' Since November, 1949, the appointment of ministers has been subject to confirmation by the government, by which their salaries are paid.[2] It includes 18 Congregations with a total membership (including the Diaspora) of 9,817.

In the U.S.A. Northern Province there are 108 Congregations and 23,529 members and adherents, or, including children, 31,817, with 14,407 scholars and teachers in the Sunday Schools.

In the U.S.A. Southern Province the numbers are 45 Congregations and 15,280 members and adherents, or, including children, 18,363, with 11,179 scholars and teachers in the Sunday Schools.

Devotion to Overseas' Missionary Work has been one of the noblest features of the Church of the Brethren. No branch of the Church of Christ has a finer story to tell than that which relates to the beginnings of the work in the West Indies, North and South America, and, particularly, in Greenland. The history

---

[1] Cf. *The Moravian Almanack and Year Book* (1954), p. 1.
[2] Ibid. p. 19.

of this work must be read elsewhere.[1] All through the years the work has been carried on with extraordinary sacrifice and perseverance. The Church of the Brethren has earned the proud right to be called *par excellence* The Missionary Church. The whole Church, and not merely a section of it, is deeply involved in this work. Few Congregations are without one or more representatives on the Mission Field. Hassé points out that whilst in the Protestant Churches at large the proportion of missionaries is about 1 to 5,000, among the Moravians it is 1 to 60.

Another important fact is that the work has to a great extent lain among primitive races, and in lands where there have been special difficulties and dangers. The Brethren were pioneers among lepers, first in Cape Colony, in 1818, and later in Jerusalem.[2]

The Missions are carried on by the Church as a whole, but the support and administration of the Mission Fields is entrusted to the several Provinces; for example, the British Province is entrusted with the care of the Mission Fields in Labrador, Eastern W. Indies with British Guiana, Jamaica, Unyamwezi and Southern Highlands (Nyasa Field) in Tanganyika, and W. Himalaya.

More details concerning the work done in the Continental Province and in the Mission Provinces and the Mission Fields may be studied in the current Almanack and Year Book.

Attention has already been made of the deep interest shown by the Brethren in the training of the young. In the sphere of general education the Church in this country is represented by three Boarding Schools, the Fulneck School for Boys, the Fulneck Girls' School, both at Fulneck, near Pudsey, Leeds, and the Ockbrook Girls' School, Ockbrook, Derby.

The whole work of the Church is directed and controlled by the General Synod. The General Directory is the standing Council of the whole Moravian Church from one General Synod to another. It consists of the Provincial Boards of the four fully self-dependent Churches. Its regular business is entrusted to an Executive Committee composed of one member

---

[1] See e.g. Cranz, op. cit. pp. 149ff.; 186ff.; 390ff.; Bost, op. cit. pp. 285ff.
[2] Cf. Hassé's, *E. R. E.*, Vol. viii., p. 839a, b.

of each of the aforesaid Boards. The Chairman of the General Directory is also the Chairman of the Executive Committee.[1]

Accepted Candidates for the Ministry are trained at the Moravian College, Fairfield, Droylsden, Manchester. Junior Students attend the Manchester University with a view to an Arts or Science Degree and Senior Students attend the lectures of the Theological Faculty with a view to a Divinity Degree.[2]

The brief account which has been given in these chapters of the origin and development of the Church of the United Brethren shows that, though much smaller than many other branches of the Church of Christ which have had a more recent origin, it has a very distinctive place in Christendom. It is episcopal, but its episcopacy is thoroughly representative and democratic. It is Scriptural and Evangelical, and its standards are those recognized by all the chief sections of the Protestant Church. It is international in its outlook and operations, as every true branch of the Church of Jesus must seek to be. It has shown itself to be adaptable to the many different situations, in various parts of the world, in which its ministries have been exercised.

Without attempting to forecast the future of this ancient Church, it may be said with confidence that its system of government, which is episcopal, but of a type which enables it to work in harmony with Churches otherwise governed; its provincial organization, enabling it to function and to adapt itself to its situation in any part of the world; its traditional friendly attitude and links with Christians of all other branches of the Evangelical Church of Christ;—all these features should enable it to make a notable contribution to the Ecumenical Movement, which is so dominant a feature of the World Christian situation to-day.

[1] Cf. *The Moravian Church Calendar and Year Book* (1954), p. 2.
[2] Ibid. p. 15.

INDEX

GEORGE ALLEN & UNWIN LTD
London: 40 Museum Street, W.C.1

Auckland: Haddon Hall, City Road
Sydney, N.S.W.: Bradbury House, 55 York Street
Cape Town: 58–60 Long Street
Bombay: 15 Graham Road, Ballard Estate, Bombay 1
Calcutta: 17 Chittaranjan Avenue, Calcutta 13
New Delhi: 13–14 Ajmere Gate Extension, New Delhi 1
Karachi: Haroon Chambers, South Napier Road, Karachi 2
Toronto: 91 Wellington Street West
Sao Paulo: Avenida 9 de Julho 1138 –Ap. 51

Thin
13 Mar. 1956.

WHAT IS RELIGION?

by Alban G. Widgery

'Probably the book of most lasting importance of all those which are before me. His book is an attempt to work out the philosophical and psychological basis of religion as it has lasting value for the minds and hearts of men. He has tried faithfully to answer the question set by his title, and readers whose prejudices are not too strong to allow them to see that there is more than one possible approach to truth will find much that is valuable and profound in Dr. Widgery's clearly written volume.'—*John O'London*

'A very fresh and readable book, careful and usually exact in its thought.'—*Christian World*

Demy 8vo   18s. net

THE LIFE OF JESUS

by Maurice Goguel

'This massive volume, with its challenging, stimulating and always sincere interpretation of the Christ . . . For those who will read it honestly and without prejudice, it will be a great experience . . . thoroughness of method, the insight, and the absolute honesty of the writer, make its perusal a liberal education.'—*Friend*

'Even those who disagree with much that the book contains will find it well worth studying.'

'His temper is at once reverent and scholarly, and his examination and presentation of the details of the story are absorbingly interesting.'—*News Chronicle*

Demy 8vo   2nd Impression   35s. net

MEN SEEKING GOD

by Christopher Mayhew, M.P.

The book describes the faith of a number of devout and representative adherents of the great religions of the world—Swami Lokeswarananda, a Hindu monk who runs a hostel for poor students in the slums of Calcutta; U San Nyun, a Buddhist layman, living near Rangoon; the Rev. Isaac Levy, Rabbi of the Hampstead Synagogue; Maulana Muhammad Ali, a Moslem prayer leader living in Lahore; Father Germanus, a Franciscan friar, and the Rev. C. C. Pande, an Indian Methodist minister who supervises a leper colony in Bengal. Each person explains his conception of God, his methods of prayer and worship, and his idea of man's destiny; and gives a selection of his favourite Scriptural quotations. In the concluding chapter Mr. Mayhew attempts a summing up. The book contains a large number of striking photographs.

Illustrated Demy 8vo   12s. 6d. net

ENCYCLOPAEDIA OF RELIGION AND RELIGIONS

by Royston Pike

'To produce a one-volume encyclopaedia of religion and religions in some 400 pages, which is really serviceable and well-informed, is something of an achievement. Mr. Royston Pike is to be congratulated on the way in which he has carried out his self-chosen task. Generally speaking, the articles, though all too brief, are fair and illuminating, we are much indebted to him for a useful book of reference.'—*Birmingham Post*

'A useful guide to ministers, teachers, and all who write on religious subjects.'—*The Christian*

Sm Roy 8vo   30s. net

GEORGE   ALLEN   &   UNWIN   LTD